The Fujifilm X-T10

**Rico Pfirstinger** studied communications and has been working as a journalist, publicist, and photographer since the mid-eighties. He has written numerous books on a diverse range of topics, from computing technology to digital desktop publishing to sled dog racing. He worked as the department head of special assignments for Hubert Burda Media in Munich, Germany, where he also served as chief editor for a winter sports website.

After eight years as a freelance film critic in Los Angeles, Rico now lives in Germany and devotes his time to digital photography and compact camera systems.

Rico writes the popular *X-Pert Corner* blog on FujiRumors. com and leads workshops called Fuji X Secrets where he offers tips and tricks on using the Fujifilm X-series cameras.

Rico Pfirstinger

# The Fujifilm X-T10

## 115 X-Pert Tips to Get the Most Out of Your Camera

rockynook

The FujiFilm X-T10
115 X-Pert Tips to Get the Most Out of Your Camera
Rico Pfirstinger
rico@ricopress.de

Project editor: Maggie Yates
Project manager: Matthias Rossmanith
Marketing: Jessica Tiernan
Copyeditor: Maggie Yates
Layout and type: Petra Strauch
Cover design: Rebecca Cowlin
Indexer: Rico Pfirstinger

ISBN: 978-1-68198-026-3
1st Edition 2016
© 2016 Rico Pfirstinger
All images © Rico Pfirstinger unless otherwise noted

Rocky Nook, Inc.
802 E. Cota Street, 3rd Floor
Santa Barbara, CA 93103
USA

www.rockynook.com

Distributed in the U.S. by Ingram Publisher Services
Distributed in the UK and Europe by Publishers Group UK

Library of Congress Control Number: 2015953475

# Table of Contents

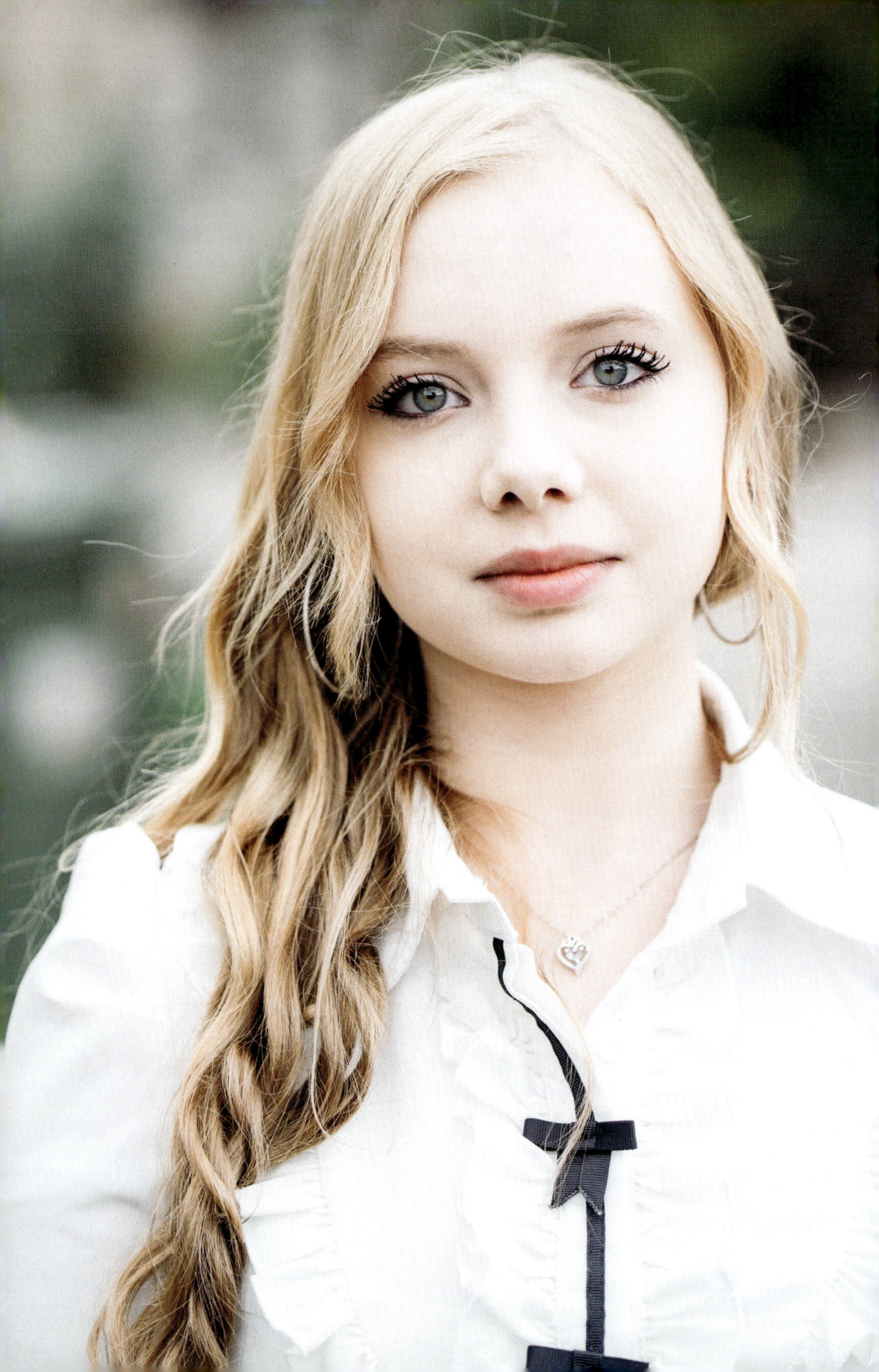

# 1. YOUR X-T10 SYSTEM

To start off, here's a brief overview of the buttons and controls on your Fujifilm X-T10:

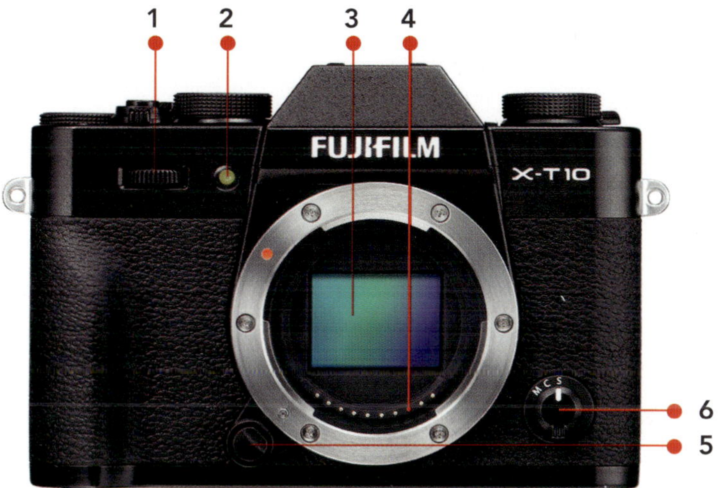

Fig. 1: **X-T10 frontal view:** front command dial with Fn button (1), AF assist lamp (2), X-Trans sensor (3), electronic lens contacts (4), lens release button (5), focus selector (6)

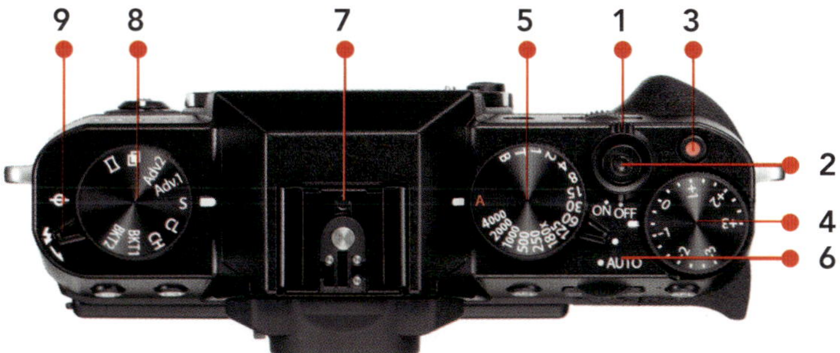

Fig. 2: **X-T10 top view:** on/off switch (1), shutter button (2), video recording button (Fn Button) (3), exposure compensation dial (4), shutter speed dial (5), AUTO switch (6), hot shoe (7), DRIVE dial (8), flash release switch (9)

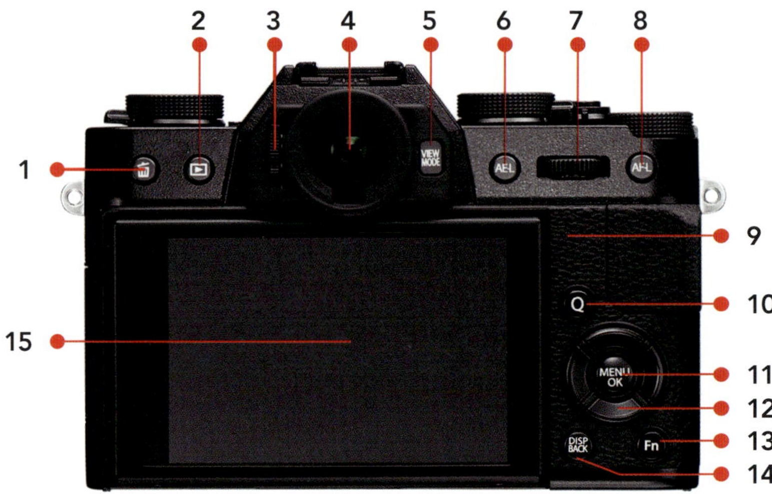

Fig. 3:  **X-T10 rear view:** delete ("trash") button (1), playback button (2), diopter adjustment dial (3), electronic viewfinder (4), view mode button (5), AE-L button (6), rear command dial with button (7), AF-L button (8), status indicator lamp (9), Q (Quick menu) button (10), MENU/OK button (11), selector keys (also rear Fn buttons) (12), rear Fn button (13), DISP/BACK button (14), tiltable LCD monitor (15)

# 1.1  THE BASICS (1): THINGS YOU SHOULD KNOW ABOUT YOUR CAMERA

**RTFM!** Read The Fuji Manual! It is included with your camera. You have a choice between the printed version and the PDF version on the CD that comes with the camera.    **TIP 1**

In case you have misplaced your printed user manual and camera CD, or you want to update to a newer edition of a manual, you can obtain downloadable PDF versions in all supported languages at this website: www.fujifilm.com/support/digital_cameras/manuals/. There, you will also find supplementary material that covers new features and changes based on firmware updates.

Please do yourself a big favor and thoroughly study this manual in order to get acquainted with the different functions of your X-T10, and don't forget that your lenses come with a user manual, as well. This book doesn't replace the X-T10 camera manual; it builds on it as an *enhancement* to the existing user manual, and offers valuable tips and background information about how to use the various features and functions of the X-T10 and make the most of your equipment.

Get a few **spare batteries**. You can buy suitable batteries either from Fujifilm or from a third party.    **TIP 2**

The X-T10 is quite a compact camera, which means that the rechargeable battery is also rather small. Depending on how you use your camera, a fully charged battery will last for 250 to 400 shots.

I recommend always setting the camera to High Performance Mode (SET-UP > POWER MANAGEMENT > HIGH PERFORMANCE > ON) in order to secure maximum autofocus and overall performance.

Please note:

- When the battery indicator changes from three to two bars, you have already used up more than half of its energy.

- When the indicator shows one remaining red bar, it's almost time to replace the battery.

Your X-T10 is using NP-W126 rechargeable batteries. This type of battery is also used in Fujifilm's X-Pro1, X-E1, X-E2, X-T1, X-M1, X-A1, and X-A2 cameras, and can be interchanged between these models.

You can obtain NP-W126 batteries from Fujifilm or compatible products from a variety of third-party vendors. Not all aftermarket batteries offer the same quality and capacity as the Fujifilm batteries, but third-party products tend to be significantly cheaper, so you can buy more of them.

If you store your camera for several days (or longer) without a charged battery, the X-T10's built-in emergency power source may run out of juice, and all camera and user settings will reset to factory conditions.

| TIP 3 | Get a suitable **battery charger** and a **travel adapter**. |

Along with spare batteries, the aftermarket also offers chargers that work with regular power outlets, USB ports, or a car's cigarette lighter jack. This way, you can charge your batteries not only at home or in your hotel room, but also on your computer's USB port or when you are traveling in a car or plane.

While traveling, don't forget that different countries use different formats for power outlets, so you may want to carry a suitable travel adapter. A particularly small and practical solution is the Apple World Travel Adapter Kit. It contains adapters for North America, Japan, China, the United Kingdom, Continental Europe, Korea, Australia, and Hong Kong. The adapters connect directly to the charger that comes with your X-T10 (no cable required). You can also use them with chargers for your Apple device (iPhone, iPad, MacBook, etc.).

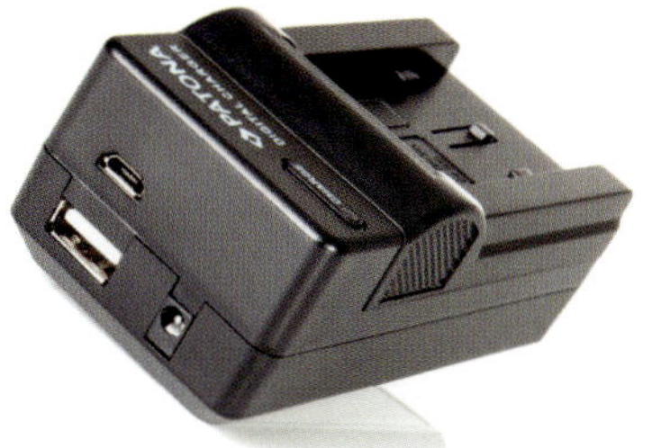

Fig. 4:
Some third-party chargers can get their power from more than one source, such as power outlets, USB ports, and car cigarette lighter jacks

Make sure that your camera and lenses are running with the latest **firmware**.        TIP 4

Fujifilm keeps improving the firmware of the X-T10 and XF/XC lenses.

- In order to check which firmware version is installed in your camera and lens, switch on the camera while pressing and holding the DISP/BACK button.

- Use the following link to find and download the latest firmware versions for your cameras and lenses: www.fujifilm.com/support/digital_cameras/software/. Here, you can also find current versions of Fuji's application software, such as RAW File Converter EX.

- A step-by-step video guide illustrating the firmware upgrade process is available here: faq.fujifilm.com/digitalcamera/faq_detail.html?id=110200895. Mac OS users can find detailed firmware download instructions here: faq.fujifilm.com/digitalcamera/faq_detail.html?id=110200803. Windows users can go to the following site: faq.fujifilm.com/digitalcamera/faq_detail.html?id=110200802.

<table>
<tr><td>TIP 5</td><td>Things to remember when updating your firmware:</td></tr>
</table>

- If you can't find a new firmware version on Fuji's firmware update page, there's a good chance that your web browser is still caching an older version of this page. In this case, either delete your browser cache or force your browser to reload the webpage from the server.

- Make sure that your computer doesn't change the name of firmware files you download due to naming conflicts caused by older firmware versions in the download folder. The correct file name of the camera firmware for your X-T10 is always FWUP0007.DAT.

- Make sure your battery is fully charged when updating your firmware.

- Always copy new firmware files for your camera or lenses into the top directory of your SD memory card, and always use cards that have been freshly formatted in your camera. After you have copied the firmware to the card, make sure to properly unmount the card from your computer before removing it.

- If you want to update the firmware for a specific lens, make sure that lens is attached to the camera when you initiate the update process.

- To start the update process for your camera or a lens, switch on the camera while pressing and holding the DISP/BACK button and follow the instructions on the screen.

- Never switch off the camera during the updating process. The camera will tell you when the update is complete. Only then can you safely switch it off.

If the firmware of your camera or lens needs to be updated due to compatibility issues, the camera will alert you of this when you switch it on. If that's the case, download the new firmware from the website links provided in tip 4 and update your camera and/or lens.

<table><tr><td>Use fast **memory cards** with at least 80 MB/s write speed.</td><td>TIP 6</td></tr></table>

Turbo-charge your camera and its built-in buffer memory by using the fastest UHS-I memory cards available. SanDisk, Lexar, Panasonic, and Toshiba offer cards with nominal write speeds of 80 MB/s or higher. *SanDisk Extreme Pro* SD cards are particularly popular among X-series photographers.

Unlike the X-T1, The X-T10 does *not* support the new and even faster UHS-II standard, which offers transmission speeds of up to 300 MB/s. Hence it's not recommended to use one of these rather expensive cards.

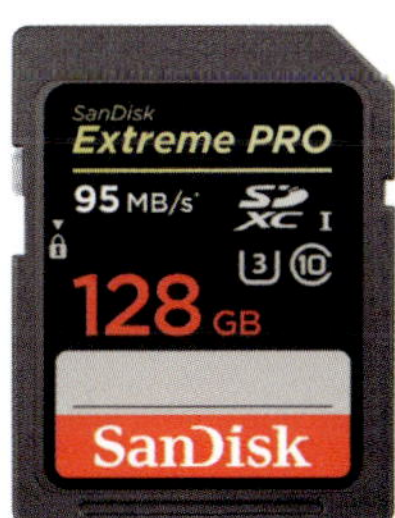

Fig. 5:
Fast **SanDisk Extreme Pro** SD memory cards with a 95 MB/s read and write speed are popular workhorses for many serious X-T10 users

<table><tr><td>Your camera is automatically numbering your images. With a little trick, you can **reset the frame counter** and even assign a new starting number.</td><td>TIP 7</td></tr></table>

Follow these steps to reset the image counter to zero:

- First select SET-UP > SAVE DATA SET-UP > FRAME NO. > RENEW, then format the SD card with SET-UP > FORMAT and take a picture. The frame counter will start from zero.

- To avoid another automatic image counter reset when you are reformatting an SD card, select SET-UP > SAVE DATA SET-UP > FRAME NO. > CONTINUOUS.

You can assign pretty much any number as the camera's new frame-counter starting number. The method is quite similar, but involves an extra step in your computer:

■ Select SET-UP > SAVE DATA SET-UP > FRAME NO. > RENEW, then format the SD card with SET-UP > FORMAT and take a picture. The frame counter will now start from zero.

■ Remove the SD card from your camera and insert it in your computer. Locate your image (for example DSCF0001. JPG or DSCF0001.RAF) in the DCIM folder and change the frame-number portion of the file name (0001) to the number you'd like to use as your new starting point. For example, you can change the file name to DSCF2000.JPG.

■ Properly unmount and remove the SD card from your computer and put the card back into your camera. Now take another picture. The camera will use the modified frame number as a starting point. In our example, the new image file's name would be DSCF2001.

■ To avoid another automatic frame-counter reset when you are reformatting an SD card, select SET-UP > SAVE DATA SET-UP > FRAME NO. > CONTINUOUS.

Please note that the X-T10 doesn't feature an internal shutter actuations counter. Image file numbers are no indication of the actual number of shots that have been taken with a particular camera and aren't a suitable measurement to gauge the wear and tear of the camera's mechanical shutter.

<table><tr><td>TIP 8</td><td>Always use **High Performance Mode!**</td></tr></table>

In its default setting, the X-T10 operates with limited performance in order to conserve power. To enjoy the camera's full capabilities, it's important to select SET-UP > POWER MANAGEMENT > HIGH PERFORMANCE > ON.

Since the X-T10 consumes more power in this mode, it's even more important to always have replacement batteries at hand.

Keep the **camera sensor** clean! TIP 9

Sooner or later, all cameras with interchangeable lenses get dust or dirt on the sensor. This manifests as spots on your image, especially in photos taken at small apertures. You can prevent this from happening by taking measures to avoid sensor dust as much as possible. You can clean dust by using your camera's built-in cleaning mechanism:

- Select SET-UP > SENSOR CLEANING > OK to activate the built-in cleaning mechanism that helps loosen dust particles. By default, this mechanism will be employed when you switch *off* the camera. I recommend setting the camera to also automatically activate this mechanism when the X-T10 is switched *on:* to do this, select SET-UP > SENSOR CLEANING > WHEN SWITCHED ON > ON.

In addition to that, it's sensible to adhere to a regime that avoids exposing the camera to dust and dirt:

- Never leave the camera without a lens or its protective body cap.

- Don't exchange lenses in dusty environments.

- When exchanging lenses, always hold the camera with the open lens mount pointed downward—never upward.

- When you attach a new lens, make sure the rear glass of the lens is clean and free of dust particles. Otherwise, dust from the lens could travel to the sensor.

- Never touch the sensor!

Fig. 6: **Dust spots** on the sensor made visible: this sensor badly needs some cleaning

<table><tr><td>TIP 10</td><td>**Do-it-yourself sensor cleaning** for tough sensor spots</td></tr></table>

When the built-in sensor-cleaning function doesn't do a proper job, you have three basic options for cleaning the sensor by yourself:

- Touchless cleaning

- Dry cleaning

- Wet cleaning

**Touchless cleaning** involves using a blower, like the *Giottos Rocket-air Blower,* to rid the sensor of dust particles. An important feature of such devices is a filter in the intake valve that prevents contaminated (dusty) air from being blown against the sensor.

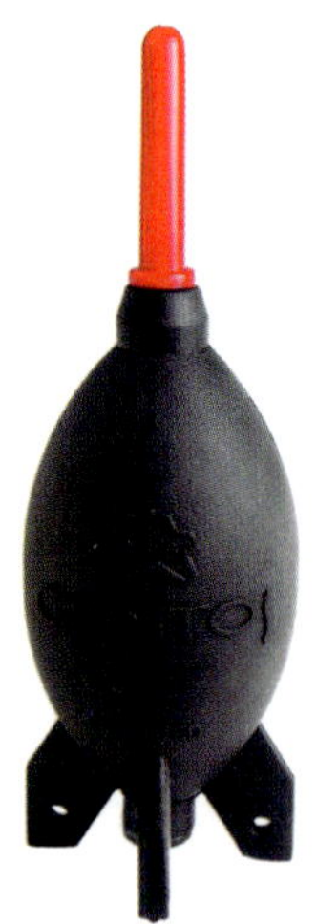

Fig. 7: Touchless sensor cleaning: **Rocket-air Blower**

***Important:*** *Don't use compressed air from aerosol cans that contain propellants. Particles could hit the sensor like tiny projectiles and damage it!*

A popular means to **dry clean** the sensor is the Pentax Sensor Cleaning Kit. The sticky head of this funny-looking cleaning device picks up dust and dirt from the sensor surface and transfers it to sticky paper sheets that are included with the product.

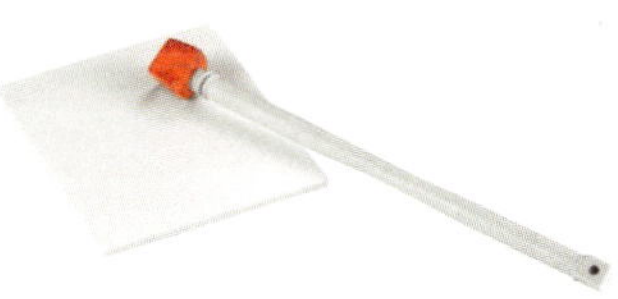

Fig. 8:
Dry cleaning: **Pentax Sensor Cleaning Kit**

Tough sensor dirt (like water or oil spots) requires wet cleaning with a *sensor swab*. Suitable products are offered by companies likes *Photographic Solutions* and *Visible Dust*. They consist of wipers that are wetted with special cleaning fluids (such as *Eclipse*). Wipe one side of the swab from left to right over the full width of the sensor, and then from right to left with the other side of the swab. Your X-T10 requires swabs that match APS-C-sized sensors. At Photographic Solutions, this translates into product size number 2.

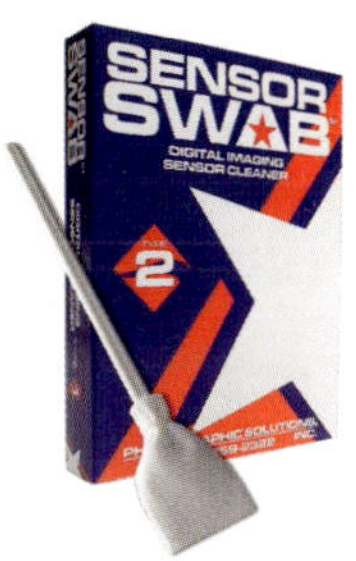

Fig. 9:
Wet cleaning: **Sensor Swab** from Photographic Solutions

Inexpensive and effective alternatives to products from Visible Dust or Photographic Solutions are APS-C-sized swabs from the Asian brand VSGO.

If some spots simply won't go away, you can always have your camera serviced and cleaned by Fujifilm. In some countries (such as Germany), the first sensor cleaning is even free of charge.

There's also a small chance that spots are caused by dust particles that are enclosed *behind* the protective surface of the sensor. In this case, the camera needs to be serviced by Fujifilm.

# 1.2 THE BASICS (2): THINGS YOU SHOULD KNOW ABOUT YOUR LENSES

Your camera is compatible with the following native X-mount lenses:

- Fujinon XF lenses (prime and zoom lenses)

- Fujinon XC lenses (compact, more affordable lenses)

- Zeiss Touit X-mount lenses (primes)

Confused about which lens category does what? Here's the lowdown as of September 2015:

- All current Fujinon zoom lenses (except for the XF16–55mmF2.8 lens) feature an optical image stabilizer (OIS).

- All Fujinon XF lenses (with the exception of the XF27mmF2.8 pancake lens) and Zeiss Touit lenses feature an aperture ring.

- XC lenses don't feature an aperture ring. With these lenses, the aperture is set using the camera's command dial.

- All Fujinon XF and XC lenses (with the exception of the XF56mm APD prime lens) support fast phase detection autofocus (PDAF) with the camera's central AF frames.

- Fujinon XF lenses offer LMO (lens modulation optimizer) support. The LMO mitigates undesirable optical effects such as diffraction, which occurs when a lens is stopped-down to a small aperture.

- Zeiss Touit lenses and Fujinon XC lenses do *not* support the LMO.

In addition to native X-mount lenses, you can also attach a host of current and older lenses from other manufacturers with the use of a suitable adapter. Remember that adapted lenses will always operate either wide open or at the set working aperture, and autofocus, program AE, and shutter priority AE are no longer available.

| XC or XF? Zoom or prime? | TIP 11 |
| --- | --- |

System cameras are mostly sold in discounted "kits" that consist of a camera body that's paired with a so-called "kit lens," which is typically a standard zoom lens with second-rate image quality.

Fujifilm is doing things a little bit differently here with the affordable and flexible XC16–50mmF3.5–5.6 OIS II kit zoom, which delivers great results. This is the second generation of the XC16–50mmF3.5–5.6 OIS kit zoom that was introduced in concert with the X-M1. The most notable improvement of the Mark II edition is its reduced minimum focus distance (MFD). This means that you can now get closer to your subject, basically adding macro capability without using an extension tube.

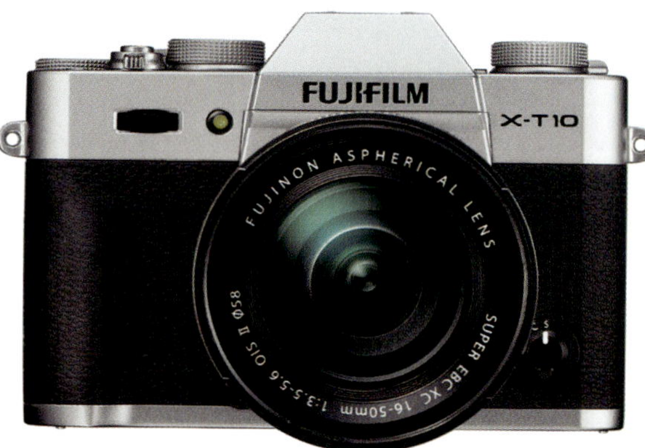

Fig. 10:  Thanks to its relatively low price, the rather compact and lightweight **XC16–50mmF3.5–5.6 OIS II** is probably the most popular kit zoom lens for the X-T10.

The XC16–50mmF3.5–5.6 OIS II is made in China with an exterior and bayonet made of less expensive plastic. To save costs, there's no aperture ring and no switch for the optical image stabilizer (OIS). With a maximum aperture of F3.5–5.6, it's also not the fastest lens on planet Earth, but make no mistake: it's built from top-notch optical glass, and the results can easily keep up with more expensive lenses.

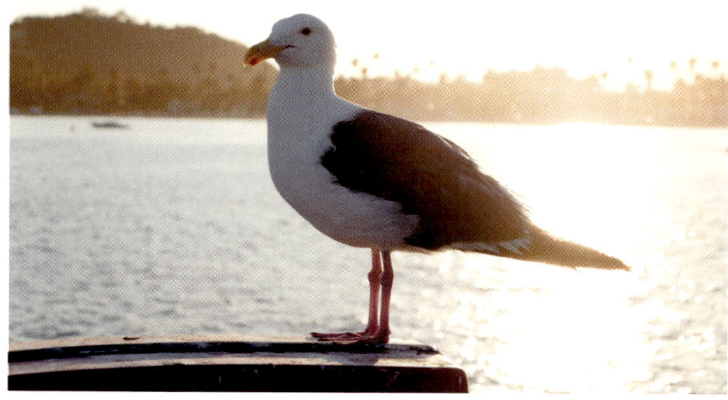

Fig. 11:  Thanks to its superior optics (relative to its low price), the **XC16–50mmF3.5–5.6 OIS II** kit zoom can master difficult shooting situations like this seagull that was shot directly against the sun.

If you are looking for a faster alternative to the affordable XC16–50mmF3.5–5.6 OIS II, the XF18–55mmF2.8–4.0 R LM OIS may be your weapon of choice. This larger, heavier kit zoom features an aperture ring and switches for OIS and aperture mode. Its build quality is very good. After years of "made in Japan," this lens is now manufactured in China, too.

To better fit this combo into your hand, you might want to consider adding an optional MHG-XT10 handgrip to the camera. Give it a try!

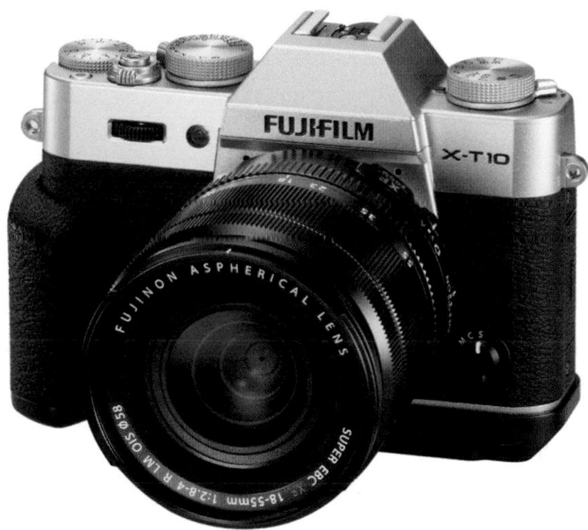

Fig. 12: The **XF18–55mmF2.8–4.0 R LM OIS** is larger, heavier, and more expensive than the XC16–50mmF3.5–5.6 OIS II. It's also faster and features an aperture ring and switches for OIS and aperture mode. This illustration shows the lens on an X-T10 in concert with an optional MHG-XT10 hand grip.

Since the X-T10 is a very compact system camera, it's a good idea to also consider a small prime lens as your standard walk-around gear. A particularly fitting choice is the small and flexible XF27mmF2.8 pancake lens. With it, the camera fits in the pocket of almost every coat or jacket. Optically, this little lens is pretty big. At 27mm (that's a full-frame equivalent of 41mm), it's very flexible and can be used for street photography, landscape (including panoramas), or even portraits with nice subject-background separation.

My recommendation: Have a closer look at the X-T10 with an XF27mm pancake lens.

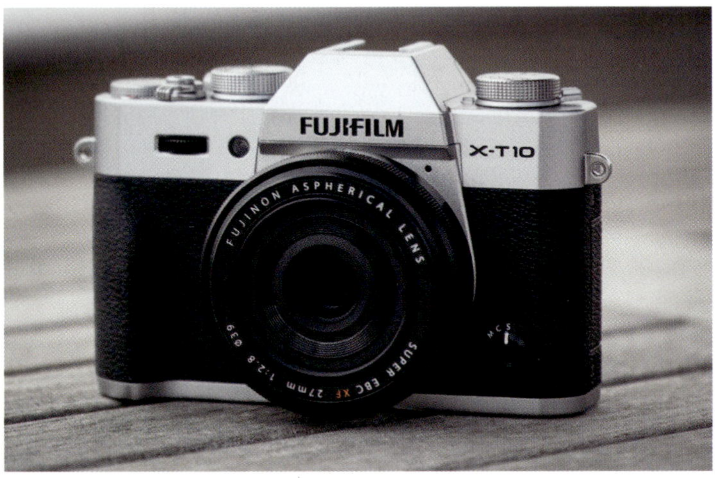

Fig. 13:  Small, but oh my! In concert with the long underestimated **XF27mmF2.8** pancake lens, the X-T10 fits in (most) coat pockets.

| TIP 12 | X-mount compatible **Samyang lenses** are just like adapted lenses! |
| --- | --- |

Manual focus lenses from Samyang (Rokinon) and similar brands aren't native X-mount lenses. They simply come with a compatible mechanical mount so you don't have to buy an additional adapter. These lenses behave like other adapted third-party lenses: they don't communicate with the camera (there's no data transmission because there aren't any electronic contacts), there's no autofocus, the live view operates with the currently set working aperture, and you can only use AE modes **A** and **M**.

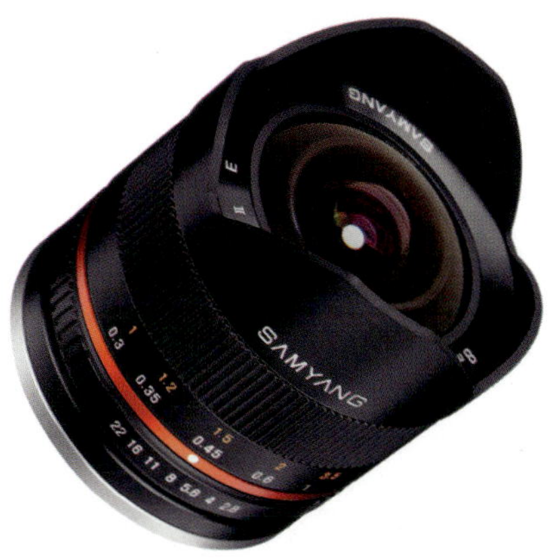

Fig. 14: The affordable **Samyang 8mmF2.8 Fisheye II** manual focus lens for Fujifilm X-mount is a popular choice to record images with extreme angles.

| **Zeiss Touit** lenses | TIP 13 |

Even though Touit lenses with native X-mount compatibility offer great image quality and work like Fujinon XF lenses, Zeiss tends to be hesitant to support new camera features with lens firmware updates. It took Zeiss about half a year longer than Fuji to offer PDAF support, and to date there is still no LMO support. There's also no indication that Zeiss wants to continue with the Touit line of lenses.

| Decoding **XF18–135mmF3.5–5.6 R LM OIS WR** | TIP 14 |

This tip is of the "what you always wanted to know but never dared to ask" variety:

- **XF:** "X" means X-mount or X-series; "F" means Fine, for Fuji's premium line of lenses. There's also the smaller, more affordable XC line ("C" stands for Compact or Casual).

- **18–135mm:** This is the focal length range of the zoom lens. To translate the numbers to their full-frame equivalents, you have to multiply them by the APS-C crop factor of 1.5. Hence, the field-of-view (FOV) of an 18–135mm zoom on your X-T10 is identical to the FOV of a 27–202mm zoom lens on a full-frame camera.

- **F3.5–5.6:** This range describes the maximum aperture opening at the low and high end of the focal-length range. In this case, the lens offers a maximum aperture of f/3.5 at 18mm and f/5.6 at 135mm.

- **R:** This stands for Ring and simply means that the lens features an aperture ring. This is a standard feature of all Fujinon XF lenses, with the exception of the XF27mmF2.8 pancake lens. XC zooms don't offer an aperture ring, either. With those lenses, the aperture setting is controlled with the rear command dial (thumb dial) when you are using exposure modes A or M.

- **LM:** This stands for Linear Motor, which ensures quick and silent autofocus operation.

- **OIS:** This is the Optical Image Stabilizer. This feature allows you to perform handheld shots at up to five stops slower of a shutter speed than you would usually need to eliminate camera shake. For example, in situations that would normally require a shutter speed of 1/80s to ensure a clear image, you could shoot with 1/4s and still get usable results. It's important to remember that motion blur often plays a role at slower shutter speeds, since many subjects tend to move. Obviously the OIS cannot reduce motion blur—only blurring that occurs due to camera shake (i.e., the shaky hands of the photographer).

- **WR** denotes weather resistant lenses. These lenses were designed with your weather resistant X-T1 in mind, but they also work with all other X-mount camera models (like your X-T10).

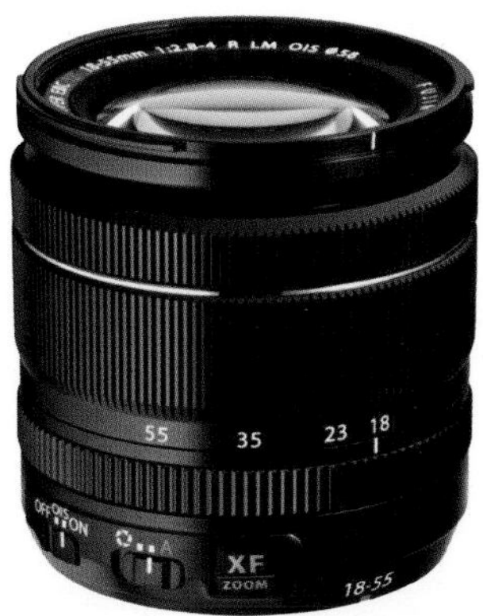


Fig. 15: The **XF18–55mmF2.8–4.0 R LM OIS** in this illustration is the more expensive of the two kit zoom options for the X-T10. It is pretty flexible and delivers very good results. A smaller and more affordable option is the XC16–50mmF3.5–5.6 OIS II zoom lens. For maximum flexibility, the larger and more expensive XF18–135mmF3.5–5.6 R LM OIS WR will do the job.

| The **optical image stabilizer (OIS)** has its quirks! | TIP 15 |
| --- | --- |

With the exception of the XF16–55mmF2.8 zoom, all XF and XC zoom lenses feature built-in optical image stabilization (OIS). Switch on the OIS to prevent camera shake and blurry images in situations that require you to take handheld shots at a slower-than-usual shutter speed. XF lenses offer a dedicated OIS on/off switch on the lens barrel. The OIS in XC lenses is controlled through a camera menu.

For handheld shots, an old rule of thumb recommends using shutter speeds that are at least as fast as the reciprocal of the full-frame-equivalent focal length that is in use. For example, with a 50mm lens and an APS-C crop factor of 1.5, the minimum safe shutter speed for handheld camera use would be *[1 / (50 × 1.5)]s = 1/75s*. In other words, when you are shooting handheld with a 50mm lens and don't want shaky images, you should use shutter speeds that are at least as fast as 1/75s. Or you can use the OIS to add a few more stops.

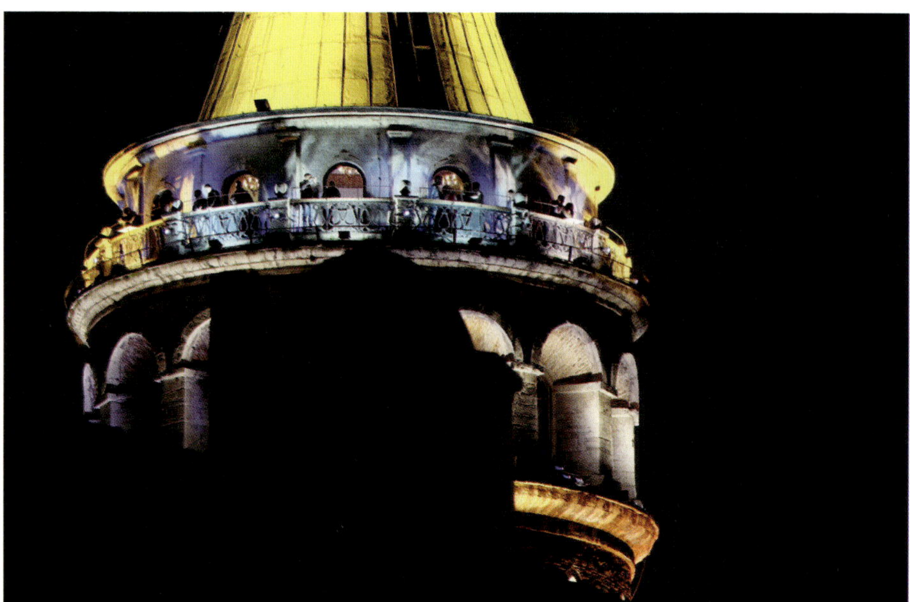

Fig. 16: The **optical image stabilizer** of the XF50–140mm in action: Thanks to a slow shutter speed of 1/6s, I could still use ISO 800 for this night shot. Even at a full-frame equivalent of 210mm, the OIS was able to successfully compensate for any camera shake caused by my hands.

Of course, rules of thumb don't apply to everybody. Some users have quite steady hands and some have rather shaky hands. The settings and equipment that work for me may not work for you. However, the OIS will always give you a few extra stops of shutter-speed headroom.

In SHOOTING MENU > IS MODE, you can choose between two basic OIS modes:

■ **OIS mode 1** (CONTINUOUS) is the default setting. It's always stabilizing the image, even when you are just looking through the viewfinder before you press the shutter button.

■ **OIS mode 2** (SHOOTING ONLY) only engages when you fully depress the shutter button to take an image.

Please note that the OIS can also *introduce* camera shake, especially at fast shutter speeds. This adverse effect is more likely to occur in OIS mode 1 than in mode 2. However, OIS mode 1 is more effective when used at very slow shutter speeds, such as 1/15s, 1/8s, or even 1/4s.

These are my recommendations for using the OIS:

- Only use (switch on) the OIS when necessary. When you are using fast shutter speeds that don't require image stabilization, you can safely turn the OIS off to eliminate it as a potential interference.

- I prefer to use the OIS in mode 2 ("shooting only"). Mode 1 is useful at very slow shutter speeds and when you are using very long focal lengths because the camera will also stabilize the live view image, making it easier to compose a shot.

- Turn off the OIS when you are working from a tripod or with shutter speeds that are slower than a second. You should also switch it off for panning shots.

By the way, the OIS emits a soft humming sound, even when the function is turned off. Don't worry about the noise.

| OIS and motion detection: what's going on? | TIP 16 |
| --- | --- |

When Auto-ISO is active and you are shooting in either aperture priority **A** or program AE **P**, the X-T10 offers another OIS option: motion detection. When the camera detects subject movement at the time of shooting, this feature increases the shutter speed by one or two stops in order to reduce unwanted motion blur. To compensate for the reduced exposure time, the camera will increase the ISO value of the shot accordingly.

Motion detection reacts on either subject movement or camera movement, which can't be compensated by the

OIS. This makes it possible to select a slower minimum shutter speed (SHOOTING MENU > ISO > AUTO (1–3) > MIN. SHUTTER SPEED) in the Auto-ISO settings, which would be suitable for static subjects. However, when the motion detection registers subject or camera movement while the shutter is half or fully depressed, it will temporarily increase the minimum shutter speed by one or two stops. It's a smart way of adapting to a quickly changing scene.

Motion detection can be combined with both OIS modes (1 and 2). You can find the option in the OIS menu (SHOOTING MENU > IS MODE) as CONTINUOUS+MOTION (= OIS mode 1 with motion detection) and SHOOTING+MOTION (= OIS mode 2 with motion detection).

Don't forget that these two additional options are only available when Auto-ISO is active and the camera is set to either aperture priority or program AE. To grant motion detection sufficient operating room, the Auto-ISO ceiling (MAX. SENSITIVITY) should be set to a reasonably high value, such as 3200 or 6400.

| TIP 17 | XF23mmF1.4 R, XF16mmF1.4 R WR and XF14mmF2.8 R are different beasts! |
|---|---|

Unlike standard X-mount lenses, the wide-angle primes **XF23mmF1.4 R, XF16mmF1.4 R WR,** and **XF14mmF2.8 R** feature a more traditional manual focus ring with a clutch mechanism:

- Pull the focus ring toward the camera to set the lens to manual focus.

- Push the focus ring away from the camera to set the lens to autofocus.

- Alternatively, you can use the traditional focus selector switch at the front of the camera to set the X-T10 to manual focus mode. In this case, the lens remains in autofocus mode, and you can only use the AF-L button

(Instant AF) to change the focus. This also means that you cannot manually adjust your focus after focusing with Instant AF.

- You cannot use Instant AF (AF-L button) to focus when the focus ring of the lens is set to manual focus. In this case, you can only use the manual focus ring to change or adjust the focus.

- As soon as you set the camera and/or the lens to manual focus, the combined electronic distance and depth-of-field (DOF) scale becomes unavailable. It simply disappears from the display, leaving you with the analog (engraved) distance and DOF markers on the lens barrel.

- The analog depth-of-field markers on the lens barrel are less conservative (and in my opinion less useful) than the camera's digital scale. This is because the camera's electronic scale is using a much smaller circle of confusion (CoC) of 0.005mm in order to display DOF ranges with pixel-sharp results at 100% magnification, whereas the engraved scale on the lens uses a value that's based on looking at typically sized prints from a typical distance with typical eyesight. Some photographers regard the engraved scale as more practical. Personally, I prefer the electronic scale. In any case, the actual difference between the two scales is about two stops. This means that in order to determine the pixel-sharp DOF for f/16 on the engraved scale, you are better off using the range that has been engraved for f/8.

- The analog distance/DOF scale is not illuminated and is hard (or even impossible) to read in dark environments. In addition to that, you have to remove the camera from your eye in order to get a current distance or DOF reading, because the digital scales are suppressed when the lens is in MF mode. It's also not possible to reverse the focusing direction of the manual focus ring with the 14mm, 16mm, or 23mm lenses (a nice feature common to all other X-series cameras and lenses).

- If you set your X-T10 to AF+MF mode (SHOOTING MENU > AUTOFOCUS SETTING > AF+MF > ON), you can only use this feature when the lens clutch is set to MF and the camera to AF-S. In this configuration, you can autofocus by half-pressing the shutter button and then manually adjust the focus with the focus ring (while keeping the shutter button half-pressed).

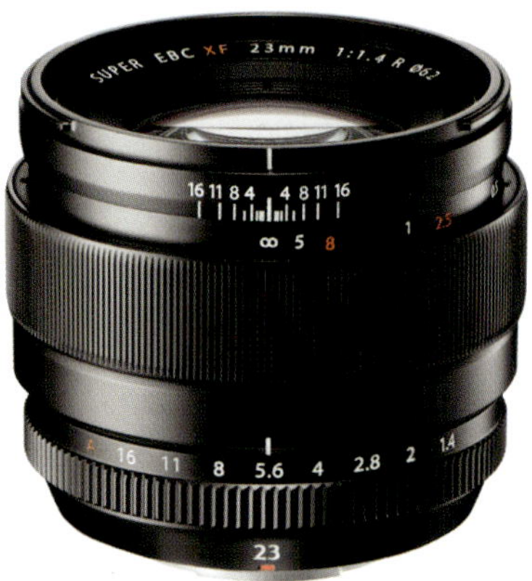

Fig. 17:  **Fujinon XF23mmF1.4 R** with engraved distance and DOF markers. It's a nice retro touch, but you lose the state-of-the-art digital functionality.

| TIP 18 | Use the **Lens Modulation Optimizer** (LMO)! |

The X-T10 supports the so-called LMO or Lens Modulation Optimizer. This feature premiered in the X100S and X20 fixed-lens cameras, and it counteracts common optical phenomena (like diffraction and corner softness) when the camera converts the RAW data into JPEG images. To make it work, the firmware in the attached lens sends the LMO correction data to the camera.

■ Neither Fujinon XC lenses nor Zeiss Touit lenses support the LMO.

If your lens supports the LMO (all Fujinon XF lenses do), you should enable the function by selecting LENS MODULATION OPTIMIZER > ON in the shooting menu.

You can also use the built-in RAW converter of your X-T10 (PLAYBACK MENU > RAW CONVERSION) to enable or disable the LMO for a specific image. With this method it is easy to create versions of a shot with and without LMO enhancements.

In its current incarnation (late 2015), the LMO takes care of the following two optical effects:

■ **Diffraction softness:** This effect increasingly occurs when the lens is stopped down beyond a certain point. APS-C cameras like the X-T10 typically exhibit diffraction at apertures of 11 and smaller. While stopping down increases the overall depth of field (DOF), it also reduces the maximum resolution of the lens/camera combination. The LMO counteracts this effect and reconstructs some of the lost detail.

■ **Corner softness:** Even the best lenses aren't as sharp in the corners as they are in the center. The LMO in the X-T10 is able to digitally compensate for that loss of quality.

LMO corrections are based on complex deconvolution algorithms. Currently, this is only supported in-camera with the built-in RAW converter. As of October 2015, external converters such as Lightroom, Adobe Camera Raw, Apple Aperture, Capture One Pro, Silkypix, Iridient Developer, Photo Ninja, and AccuRaw can't process LMO data. This means that LMO corrections are only visible in JPEGs that are generated in the camera.

| TIP 19 | Things you should know about **digital lens corrections** |

Most modern lenses achieve their optimal image quality through a combination of optical and digital corrections. Corrections are mostly applied to the three following phenomena:

- **Vignetting:** This effect results in a loss of brightness from center to corner. Vignetting is more pronounced at large apertures.

- **Distortion:** There are pincushion- and barrel-type distortions, both of which make straight lines seem curved. Premium primes like the XF14mm, XF23mm, XF35mmF1.4, XF56mm, and XF90mm are fully optically corrected for distortion. Others (such as the Zeiss Touit range, compact pancake lenses, the XF35mmF2, or zoom lenses) require a combination of optical and digital distortion correction.

- **Chromatic aberration:** Chromatic aberration results in color fringing. This effect can be corrected (or mitigated) with apochromatic lenses or digitally corrected during RAW conversion.

Some camera makers rely on dedicated correction profiles that have to be provided by each RAW converter maker. Fujifilm isn't one of these companies: all current Fujifilm cameras store digital corrections as metadata in the RAW file. RAW converters can access this lens-specific metadata and use it to apply appropriate corrections. This way, the built-in RAW converter and external software, such as Lightroom, Aperture, Silkypix, Iridient Developer, or Capture One, can use the metadata in the RAW file to correct or mitigate vignetting, distortion, and chromatic aberration.

A major benefit of this method is that many RAW converters automatically support new lenses since Fujifilm delivers the correction data via the RAW metadata. However, there's also a drawback: some RAW converters (such as Lightroom,

Adobe Camera Raw, Aperture, and Silkypix) don't give you the option to switch off metadata-based digital lens corrections, even if you're convinced they aren't necessary. Since digital distortion correction always results in some loss of image sharpness and detail due to the required stretching and interpolation, this can be a headache for some users. Obviously, not all subjects or images require the same amount of digital correction (it can also be a simple matter of taste), so full user control over the application of digital lens corrections is a very nice feature.

Luckily, software like Iridient Developer and Capture One offer full control over how much digital metadata distortion (or vignetting) correction should be applied. Other programs (like Photo Ninja, Raw Photo Processor/RPP, and AccuRaw) simply ignore lens correction metadata. With such programs, all corrections have to be applied either manually or by using a dedicated profile.

| Use the included **lens hood**! | TIP 20 |
|---|---|

With the single exception of the XF27mmF2.8 pancake lens, all Fujifilm XF and XC lenses come with a fitted lens hood, which should be used whenever possible. Apart from its optical benefits, the hood protects the lens and the front glass element from damage.

Lens hoods can pose problems, too: they make the lens appear bigger than it actually is, and they can shade the camera flash or the autofocus assist light. They also use up extra space in your bag, although most hoods can be reverse-mounted on the lens for transport purposes.

When you shoot with a small shoe-mounted flash, or when you depend on using the AF assist lamp, it's best to remove the lens hood.

---

**TIP 21** | Lens protection filters—yes or no?

---

Digital cameras like the X-T10 don't require the UV or skylight filters that used to be very popular in the days of analog film photography. This means that a permanently affixed filter has no optical purpose, and only serves as protective glass. This additional glass can have a negative effect on image quality, especially at night and when you shoot against a bright light source. Filters increase the chance of ghosting, unwanted reflections, or a loss of contrast.

This is why I recommend using protective glass only in situations that actually require this additional protection layer. In most situations, the lens hood should provide sufficient protection. If you still decide to use a filter, make sure to choose a high-quality product. Fujifilm offers suitable protective filters that feature the same Super EBC coating used on all of their XF/XC lenses. Be prepared to pay a premium, though.

---

**TIP 22** | **39mm filters** can be tricky!

---

The **XF60mmF2.4 R** and **XF27mmF2.8** lenses require filters with a 39mm thread. It's important that those filters are designed in a way that allows the inner lens barrel to freely retract into the outer barrel while the filter is attached. If this isn't possible (for example, because a thin step-up ring is directly attached to the lens or because the filter's overall diameter is too large), the lens can be damaged when the filter or step-up ring collides with the outer barrel of the lens.

A typical indicator for this and other mechanical lens problems is a message alerting you that the camera needs to be switched off and on again. A possible solution is putting a spacer (a suitable 39mm filter, for example) between the lens and the step-up ring. You should remove the glass from the spacer, so any cheap/old/unused 39mm filter will do the job as long as it fits and doesn't interfere with the outer lens barrel when the inner barrel is retracting.

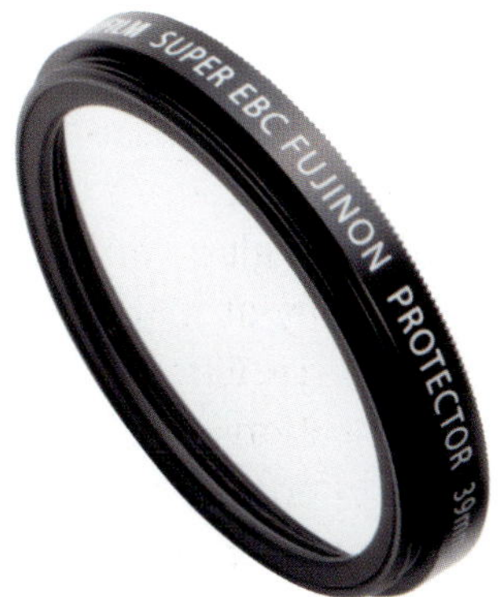

Fig. 18:  A **39mm protection filter** by Fujifilm. A filter like this can also be used as a spacer between the lens (XF60 or XF27) and a step-up ring.

# 1.3 THE BASICS (3): USEFUL ACCESSORIES

There's a rich selection of accessories for your X-T10. Whether or not you believe such add-ons are useful, I'll cover a few select items that can, in my opinion and experience, improve the functionality of your camera.

| Optional handgrip | TIP 23 |
|---|---|

An optional handgrip can improve the ergonomics of the X-T10 when you are using large, heavy lenses or if you have large hands.

The **MHG-XT10** offers a tripod mount on the optical axis, provides full access to the battery compartment, and is compatible with Arca-Swiss-type tripod heads, so you don't need a dedicated quick release plate. The handgrip *is* the quick release plate.

Fig. 19:  The optional **handgrip MHG-XT10** provides direct access to the battery compartment and can be mounted on an Arca-Swiss-type tripod head

| TIP 24 | **Off-camera TTL flash** with a Canon OC-E3 TTL extension cord |
| --- | --- |

Basically, the X-T10 can be combined with most third-party flashes, as long as the flash output is controlled manually. However, Fuji's automated TTL flash exposure (called Super Intelligent Flash in a grossly exaggerated fashion) currently only works with Fujifilm compatible TTL flash units like the **EF-20, EF-X20,** and **EF-42,** or the new **Nissin i40**. There's also a small Metz flash offering Fujifilm TTL support: the **mecablitz 26 AF-1 digital**.

TTL is an abbreviation for "Through The Lens," which means that the camera determines the appropriate flash output by measuring a scene through the lens with a weak preflash. In order to work in TTL mode, TTL flash units have to be connected with the camera's hot shoe, and strangely enough, there's still no Fujifilm-branded TTL extension cable on the market that would allow you to use a TTL flash off-camera. A simple solution is using a **Canon OC-E3** extension cable, because it's pin-compatible with Fuji's own flash contacts. With such a cable (or a compatible third-party product), it is possible to use an EF-20, EF-X20, or EF-42 off-camera in TTL mode. Please note that Canon OC-E3 cables are only compatible with Fuji's TTL flash *connectors,* not with Fuji's TTL flash *protocol.* This means that it isn't possible to use Canon TTL flash units with an X-T10 in TTL mode. The protocols won't match. You can still use them in manual mode, though.

Fujifilm's compact (and retro-styled) EF-X20 flash features an optical slave mode and can be wirelessly triggered by another flash unit. However, this is no automated TTL mode, so the output of the EF-X20 has to be manually controlled while in slave mode.

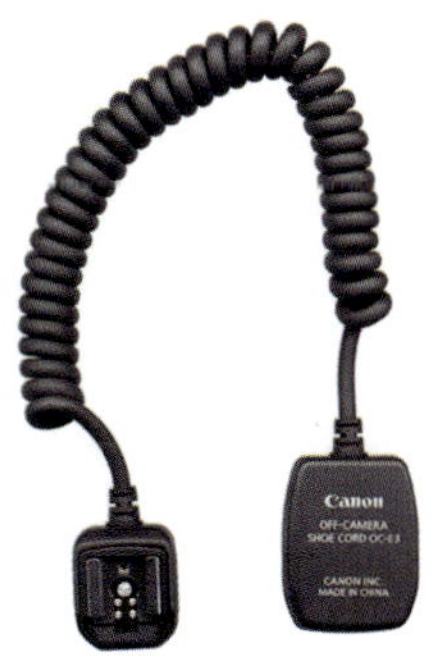


Fig. 20:
A **Canon-compatible TTL extension cord** also works with the X-T10

<table><tr><td>**Remote shutter release:** three options for the X-T10</td><td>TIP 25</td></tr></table>

Now and then you may encounter situations that require you to remotely release the shutter without vibration. A quick-and-dirty method is using the camera's self-timer with a delay of either two or ten seconds, although a better way is using a remote shutter release. Your X-T10 features three different ports to connect remote shutter releases:

■ A **mechanical thread** on the shutter button allows you to connect a traditional cable release.

- There's an **RR-90 port** (Micro-USB port) that is compatible with a variety of electronic remote controls.

- You can connect electronic remote shutter releases to the camera's **microphone port** (a 2.5mm input).

Electronic shutter releases are available in tethered and wireless versions. Wireless options always consist of a transmitter and a receiver. The transmitter sends a trigger signal that is picked up by the receiver, which triggers the camera with an electronic cable that's connected to the RR-90 or microphone port.

Fujifilm offers a simple RR-90-compatible shutter release cable, but there are more sophisticated (both tethered and wireless) solutions from third parties, such as programmable intervalometers.

If you already own an older RR-80-type shutter release (which was the standard for the X-E1), you can buy a third-party adapter cable that lets you use RR-80 remote shutter releases with RR-90 cameras. Please note that a simple USB adapter doesn't work; you have to ask for a dedicated RR-80 to RR-90 adapter.

The microphone port of the X-T10 is compatible with a widely used Canon remote shutter release standard. Among others, it is compatible to the following camera models: Canon EOS Digital Rebel, Canon EOS 1000D, Canon EOS 100D, Canon EOS 1100D, Canon EOS 300D, Canon EOS 350D, Canon EOS 400D, Canon EOS 450D, Canon EOS 500D, Canon EOS 550D, Canon EOS 600D, Canon EOS 60D, Canon EOS 60Da, Canon EOS 650D, Canon EOS 700D, Canon EOS Kiss Digital, Canon EOS Kiss F, Canon EOS Kiss Digital N, Canon EOS Kiss X2, Canon EOS Kiss X3, Canon EOS Kiss X4, Canon EOS Kiss X5, Canon EOS Kiss X50, Canon EOS Kiss X6i, Canon PowerShot G1 X, Canon PowerShot G10, Canon PowerShot G11, Canon PowerShot G12, Canon PowerShot G15, Canon PowerShot SX50 HS, Canon EOS Rebel SL1, Canon EOS Rebel T1i, Canon EOS Rebel 70 T2i, Canon EOS Rebel

T3, Canon EOS Rebel T3i, Canon EOS Rebel T4i, Canon EOS Rebel XS, Canon EOS Rebel XSi, Canon EOS Rebel XT, Canon EOS Rebel XTi, Canon EOS Rebel T5i, Contax 645, Contax N, Contax N Digital, Contax N1, Contax NX, Hasselblad H1, Hasselblad H3D, Hasselblad H4D-200MS, Hasselblad H4D-31, Hasselblad H4D-40, Hasselblad H4D-50, Hasselblad H4D-50MS, Hasselblad H4D-60, Pentax 645D, Pentax *ist D, Pentax *ist DL, Pentax *ist DL2, Pentax *ist DS, Pentax *ist DS2, Pentax K-30, Pentax K-5, Pentax K-7, Pentax K-m, Pentax K10 Grand Prix, Pentax K100D, Pentax K100D Super, Pentax K10D, Pentax K110D, Pentax K200D, Pentax K20D, Pentax MZ-6, Pentax MZ-L, Pentax ZX-L, Samsung GX-1L, Samsung GX-1S, Samsung GX-20, Samsung NX10, Samsung NX100, Samsung NX11, Samsung NX5, Sigma SD1, Sigma SD1 Merrill, and Sigma SD15.

This list isn't complete, but it's a pretty good start. Remote shutter releases that are compatible with any of these listed cameras should also work with the your X-T10.

Triggertrap Mobile is a smart and flexible way to trigger cameras with a smartphone (Android or iOS). In order to make it work with an X-T10, you need a dongle and an adapter cable. You can read more about this on Triggertrap's official website: www.triggertrap.com.

Of course, you can also remote control the camera using its built-in Wi-fi function and the free Fujifilm Camera Remote app for iOS or Android devices (found here: app.fujifilm-dsc.com/en/camera_remote/index.html).

# 2. USING THE FUJIFILM X-T10

## 2.1 READY, SET, GO!

New users often ask about how to achieve the perfect settings for their camera. Short answer: there are no perfect
settings. If they existed, Fuji could have saved us the trouble
of navigating the menu options and simply implemented
those ideal settings as the factory default.

Obviously, this short answer isn't satisfactory to readers
of this book, so here's a longer one:

- Years of practical experience with digital Fujifilm cameras have lead me to suggest a set of recommended basic
  settings that are meant to provide good overall performance and as much flexibility as possible.

- Many settings (such as film simulation modes, color saturation, contrast, sharpness, noise reduction, etc.) belong
  in the "JPEG settings" category. They don't affect the RAW
  files, only the out-of-camera JPEGs that are generated
  during RAW conversion. These settings aren't global or
  camera-specific—they are image-specific and each image should be adjusted individually.

- In addition to the recommended standard settings, there
  are a number of shortcuts and key combinations that
  can make choosing the optimal camera settings for any
  situation much easier.

<table><tr><td>AUTO mode: two cameras in one body</td><td>TIP 26</td></tr></table>

Your X-T10 contains two cameras for the price of one:

- A "real" camera with plenty of functions, buttons, and dials that can easily keep up with the more expensive X-T1

- An "idiot-proof" camera with automated scene recognition and a healthy selection of scene modes that assume almost all responsibility from the photographer

Which of these two cameras do you want to use? It all depends on the setting of the AUTO switch on the X-T10's top plate.

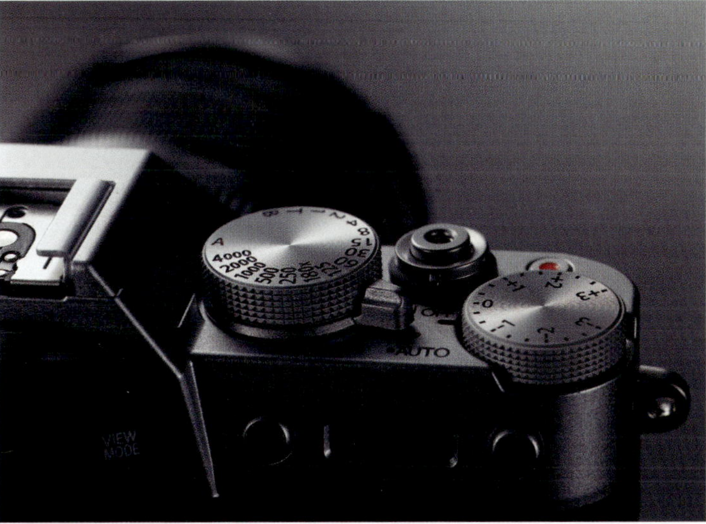

Fig. 21: The **AUTO switch** turns your X-T10 into a fully automated camera with scene recognition and scene modes. In AUTO mode, many functions and settings are either limited or no longer available in order to simplify the picture-taking process. For example, the camera automatically chooses aperture, shutter speed, and ISO settings. The exposure compensation dial is still available, though, and the majority of scene modes still allow you to focus manually as an option.

Since you are reading a book with X-Pert tips on mastering the X-T10, you'll probably be using your camera in its "regular" mode. As a photo enthusiast, you want to know how things actually work and how to make them work for you.

However, you may not be the only person who's using your X-T10. Sometimes you might want to hand it to strangers so they can take a snapshot of you. Maybe you have family members, friends, or colleagues who also want to use the camera, but don't have the time or inclination to read the manual or this book. In such cases, AUTO mode can be your friend—it makes it easy to take pictures of reasonable quality without mastering the camera's many functions.

In AUTO mode, your X-T10 records only JPEGs; no RAW files. It's controlled via the rear command dial, which allows you to pick either SR+ (ADVANCED SCENE RECOGNITION AUTO) or one of 14 so-called SCENE POSITION (SP) modes:

- SR+ (ADVANCED SCENE RECOGNITION AUTO) is a fully automated scene recognition mode that analyzes the scene and automatically picks an appropriate scene mode (such as portrait, night scene, or macro).

- The 14 dedicated scene modes deliver more-or-less intelligent presets to deal with specific shooting situations. You can choose between PORTRAIT, PORTRAIT ENHANCER, LANDSCAPE, SPORT, NIGHT, NIGHT (TRIPOD), FIREWORKS, SUNSET, SNOW, BEACH, UNDERWATER, PARTY, FLOWER, and TEXT.

SR+ and the 14 dedicated scene modes automatically control aperture, shutter speed, and ISO settings. However, you can still use the exposure compensation dial in SR+ and in all scene modes (with the exception of FIREWORKS). This means that you can adjust the brightness of your image (its exposure) as you please.

Autofocus is rather limited in the camera's AUTO mode: it only operates in ZONE mode with a central 5×3 matrix that can't be moved around. Some modes (like PORTRAIT) always activate face detection, while some (like PARTY) allow you to switch it on or off as you please. When face detection is active, you can also add the eye detection option by selecting SHOOTING MENU > AUTOFOCUS SETTING > EYE DETECTION AF and picking one of the settings. Manual focus is also available in many scene position modes.

You can find a full account of which functions are available (or not available) in each scene position mode in the appendix titled "Restrictions on Camera Settings" in the X-T10 user manual, starting at page 152.

| | |
|---|---|
| Scene Position modes comparison—ready-to-use recipes for less experienced users | **TIP 27** |

The 14 different scene modes of your X-T10 are tailored to specific shooting situations, though you shouldn't overestimate the camera's intelligence. There's a reason why the exposure compensation dial is fully functional even in the fully automated SR+ setting. It means that even the most inexperienced user is supposed to take care of the correct brightness (exposure) of an image, instead of leaving this task to the camera.

As mentioned in the previous tip, the appendix of the X-T10 user manual contains a list of functions that are (or aren't) available in SR+ or any specific scene mode. In addition to that, I'd like to give you a brief overview of some scene mode specifics:

- PORTRAIT is for images of persons. It always works with autofocus, and uses face detection (and optional eye detection) to accurately focus on human faces. Your X-T10 is using this scene mode with a minimum ISO setting of 400, which indicates that a dynamic range (DR) setting of DR200% is used to add an extra stop of highlight dynamic range. This makes perfect sense, since (especially female) faces should be exposed brightly in order to look attractive. However, shooting with the camera's standard DR100% setting can easily lead to blown highlights or unwanted skin reflections. DR200% expands the highlight dynamic range by one stop, reducing such unwanted effects in the resulting JPEG image. In other words: bright skin tones are compressed by exposing them brightly in concert with DR200%, which reduces blemishes and reflections in the process. You can also use a (fill-in) flash in PORTRAIT mode. In this case, the X-T10 will fire a preflash to reduce the unwanted red-eye effect. DR200% will also help when the flash is used by protecting the bright parts of the face against overexposure.

- PORTRAIT ENHANCER works very much like PORTRAIT mode, but adds skin softening to the final image, giving faces a waxy, doll-like look. Like PORTRAIT mode, it's best to use the exposure compensation dial to make sure that faces are brightly exposed.

- LANDSCAPE is a mode for landscape shots (who'd have thought?). It uses a custom daylight white balance setting. This mode supports AF-S and AF-C autofocus and manual focusing.

- SPORT is meant for fast moving subjects, so the X-T10 prefers fast shutter speeds. It is particularly useful in concert with burst mode settings (CL or CH on the DRIVE dial).

- NIGHT is a mode for handheld shooting in low light, typically after the sun has set. In this mode, the camera's Auto-ISO will go up to 3200 in order to realize sufficiently fast shutter speeds.

- NIGHT (TRIPOD) is the sibling mode of NIGHT, and is used for night shots taken from a tripod. Here, automatic ISO is limited to settings between 200 and 400, resulting in slow shutter speeds that can only be useful when the camera is operated from a tripod or sitting on a stable surface. To mitigate camera shake, you should use the self-timer (2 sec. delay) or a remote shutter release. Since this mode doesn't automatically disable the optical image stabilizer (OIS), you should manually switch it off.

- FIREWORKS closes the aperture down to 16 or 22 (depending on the lens) and exposes the image for 2 seconds at ISO 200 using a warm white balance. Autofocus is set to infinity, but you can also use manual focusing (MF) if you like. Of course, it's best to use FIREWORKS mode from a tripod. Again, the OIS isn't automatically turned off, so you should manually switch it off.

- SUNSET uses a warm white balance in concert with underexposure to achieve warm and saturated colors.

- SNOW uses daylight white balance, but there's no visible positive exposure compensation to make snow look brighter. This means that it's the user's job to apply sufficient exposure compensation (using the exposure compensation dial) to make snowfields look white.

- BEACH works just like SNOW. It's optimized for sunny, brightly lit vacation scenes.

- UNDERWATER is suitable for underwater shots while snorkeling or diving and applies a white balance setting that compensates for the bluish tint of underwater lighting. This scene mode can also be used in zoo aquariums with very large tanks to take pictures of fish that are swimming in bluish surroundings.

- PARTY is optimized for interior shots with incandescent light, but you can still add some flash light to the scene if you want.

- FLOWER is a mode for closeup and macro photography.

- TEXT can be used to take pictures of correspondence when there's no scanner or copy machine in reach. Please note that some positive exposure compensation may be necessary to make sure that white sheets of paper actually appear as white in the resulting JPEG image.

| TIP 28 | **Recommended settings** for your X-T10 |
|---|---|

There is no perfect set of basic camera settings that could suit all users in all situations. However, the following settings will allow you to use the X-T10 in a flexible manner with good overall performance:

- This book assumes that you are using the X-T10 in its **regular shooting mode,** not in AUTO mode. However, the following recommended settings can also be useful to AUTO mode users, since some settings will also be recognized in SR+ or different Scene Position modes.

- **Auto-ISO** is a convenient option with three presets that can be selected with SHOOTING MENU > ISO > AUTO(1–3). The corresponding Auto-ISO fine-tuning is available for each Auto-ISO preset by pressing the right selector button. There, you can adjust DEFAULT SENSITIVITY (I suggest 200), MAX. SENSITIVITY (I suggest 6400) and MIN. SHUTTER SPEED. Don't worry: even at the upper limit of ISO 6400, the results of the X-Trans sensor are quite good. When you are using Auto-ISO, you should pick a suitable minimum shutter speed with MIN. SHUTTER SPEED. A popular setting for the minimum shutter speed is 1/60s, but you can change this parameter to anything between 1/4s and 1/500s. Using a stabilized (OIS) lens, speeds slower than 1/60s are definitely realistic. With fast-moving objects, faster speeds are recommended to avoid unwanted motion blur. My personal minimum shutter speed settings for AUTO1, AUTO2, and AUTO3 are 1/60s (landscape), 1/160s (portraits), and 1/500s (action).

- Always select **FINE+RAW** under SHOOTING MENU > IMAGE QUALITY or in the Quick menu. This will get you high-resolution out-of-camera JPEGs (digital prints) *and* flexible RAW files (digital negatives). Using the RAW files, you can create a variety of diverse JPEGs with different looks and settings using the camera's built-in RAW converter (PLAYBACK MENU > RAW CONVERSION). Specifically, you can adjust JPEG parameters such as white balance, film simulations, contrast, brightness, noise reduction, and color saturation. This enables you to create different versions of a shot from a single RAW file; for example, you can make both color and black-and-white versions of the same image, including different contrast settings. You don't have to worry about choosing the perfect JPEG settings prior to taking a shot because you can always change and optimize those settings after the fact in the camera's internal RAW converter.

- As a typical standard setting, most photographers use **single shot drive** (set the DRIVE dial to the S position) and **single shot autofocus** (AF-S; select S with the focus selector at the front of the camera).

- The most flexible AF-S setting is **Single Point AF** (SHOOTING MENU > AUTOFOCUS SETTING > AF MODE > SINGLE POINT). This mode allows you to select the area of the image on which the camera should be focused. To accomplish this, press the AF button (usually the arrow-down selector key) or select SHOOTING MENU > AUTOFOCUS SETTING > FOCUS AREA, then use the selector keys (arrow keys) to pick one of the 49 available AF frames. You can change the size of the selected AF frame by turning a command dial. *Pressing* (not turning) the rear command dial resets the frame to its default size. Pressing the DISP/BACK button selects the central (default) AF frame. Press OK or half-press the shutter button to confirm your selection. The camera will use this frame in AF-S and AF-C modes as its focus area as soon as you press or half-press the shutter button.

- Unlike most DSLR cameras, the X-T10 uses a **hybrid auto-focus system:** a blend of contrast detection autofocus (CDAF) and phase detection autofocus (PDAF). The main burden still rests on the CDAF, which covers all AF frames (almost the entire sensor area). The PDAF is only covered by the central AF frames. It is faster, but potentially less precise, and it only works in sufficiently good light. Both AF methods work most precisely with a small AF frame, but work faster and more reliably with a large AF frame. This leads to an obvious conflict of interest. My basic AF frame size rule is: always select an AF frame that is as large as possible, but as small as necessary.

- Set your X-T10 to maximum performance by selecting SET-UP > POWER MANAGEMENT > HIGH PERFORMANCE > ON. This option is *not* enabled by default, so you have to manually select it. Only **high-performance mode** unleashes the full potential of the camera. This mode also uses up more energy, so make sure to always carry one or two fully charged replacement batteries.

- To further improve AF performance, you can select SHOOTING MENU > AUTOFOCUS SETTING > PRE-AF > ON. **Pre-AF** makes the camera focus on whatever is covered by the currently selected AF frame or zone, even when the shutter button is *not* pressed or half-pressed. This can save valuable split seconds when you actually take a shot, but it also means that the camera is using up more energy. Worse, in this mode the lens is always focusing on something, so it may make distracting noises. For these reasons, I *don't* recommend using Pre-AF as your default setting. Only use it under special circumstances.

- Set SHOOTING MENU > AUTOFOCUS SETTING > RELEASE/ FOCUS PRIORITY to FOCUS for both AF-S and AF-C. **Focus**

**Priority** makes sure that the camera records a picture only when the autofocus thinks that it has locked onto a target. In RELEASE mode, the X-T10 will take the shot even if the autofocus couldn't find a lock. Please note that if you are using AF+MF mode, AF-S will always operate with release priority. My recommended default setting for SHOOTING MENU > AUTOFOCUS SETTING > AF+MF is ON.

- If you want to quickly take a series of single shots, I recommend selecting SET-UP > SCREEN SET-UP > IMAGE DISP. > OFF in order to not interrupt your flow. However, I *normally* set **Image Display** to 0.5 SEC, because I like to see a quick preview of the final image that represents the camera's dynamic range (DR) settings. To cancel an ongoing image preview and continue shooting, simply half press the shutter button.

- By pressing the DISP/BACK button, you can choose between two live view display modes: one with and one without an information overlay. The overlay option offers essential tools like the electronic level, the live histogram, or the electronic distance and DOF scale. To choose which elements you want displayed, select SET-UP > SCREEN SET-UP > DISP. CUSTOM SETTNG and pick the desired elements from the list. Make sure to enable the live histogram! Personally, I select *all* available options in this menu. Please note that you can select the display mode *independently* for the EVF and the LCD. Pressing the DISP/BACK button only affects the currently active view (either the EVF or the LCD). In order to change the display mode of the EVF, the EVF must be active when you press the DISP/BACK button—for example, by looking through the viewfinder while the eye sensor is active.

- Use the VIEW MODE button to activate the **eye sensor,** which will automatically switch the camera between EVF and LCD depending on which view is in use. There's also an alternative mode called EVF ONLY + EYE SENSOR, which is an energy-saving mode. This mode can make it more difficult to use the camera, because the LCD isn't available for changing menus while in shooting mode.

- For **exposure metering,** I recommend using MULTI as your default mode. Intelligent matrix metering usually delivers results that don't require a massive amount of exposure correction. You can select the metering mode with SHOOTING MENU > PHOTOMETRY in the Quick menu, or by assigning this function to an Fn button.

- Set SHOOTING MENU > WHITE BALANCE > AUTO to let the camera set the correct **white balance** for a scene. Since you are shooting FINE+RAW, you can always adjust the white balance later, either with the camera's built-in RAW converter or with external RAW conversion software such as Adobe Lightroom. That said, AUTO will deliver very good results in most scenarios.

- If you want to keep things very simple, I recommend selecting SHOOTING MENU > DYNAMIC RANGE > AUTO as your default setting. This enables the X-T10 to automatically determine whether or not a scene requires an extra stop of **dynamic range** (DR). In this mode, the camera either shoots the scene in DR100% (standard mode) or in DR200% (with an extra stop of dynamic range in the highlights). Please note that DR400% (for *two* extra stops of dynamic range in the highlights) is only available by manual selection, not in DR AUTO mode. Extending the dynamic range maintains the texture in the bright areas of your shot (such as white clouds on a sunny day) and prevents them from appearing blown out.

- To use **adapted lenses** with your X-T10, you need either Fujifilm's Leica M adapter or a suitable third-party adapter. In order to make third-party adapters work, you have to select SHOOTING MENU > SHOOT WITHOUT LENS

> ON. This is necessary because adapted lenses (and third-party lens adapters) do not feature electronic X-mount contacts, so the lens will not register as being connected to the camera. When you are working with an adapted lens, you should also enter its focal length in SHOOTING MENU > MOUNT ADAPTOR SETTING. This ensures that the EXIF data will show the proper focal length.

■ Do you sometimes shoot with very slow shutter speeds lasting several seconds? In this case, I recommend setting SHOOTING MENU > LONG EXPOSURE NR > ON to improve the quality of your results. In this mode, the X-T10 performs a so-called dark-frame subtraction to reduce noise and eliminate hot pixels. By doing so, the total exposure time is doubled, because the camera is taking the shot twice: once normally and once with a closed shutter curtain. The second shot is then subtracted from the first to improve the overall result.

| Avoiding the camera menus: **practical shortcuts** for your X-T10 | TIP 29 |
| --- | --- |

Navigating nested camera menus can be cumbersome. That's why the X-T10 offers the Quick menu (Q button) and user-configurable Fn keys that provide direct access to important and frequently used camera functions and settings.

Beyond that, the X-T10 also offers seven custom user settings (C1 through C7) that can hold sets of frequently used camera settings. You can select one of these sets (or profiles) via the Quick menu or an appropriately configured Fn key. By doing so, you can overwrite the current camera settings with one of the seven custom user profiles. This means that C1 through C7 aren't camera *modes,* they are just memory locations that conveniently store whole sets of camera settings. They are simple shortcuts to immediately change your current camera settings to a predefined set of options.

Speaking of shortcuts—there are more of them, and most of them are available at your fingertips:

- Pull up the Quick menu, then press and hold the Q button again for a few seconds to directly open the configuration menu for your custom user settings (C1 to C7).

- Press and hold the Q button while the Quick menu is *not* open to directly access the Quick menu configuration page. In this mode, you can *customize* the Quick menu to meet your personal requirements. You can assign one of 27 different settings to any of the 16 available Quick menu elements. If you don't need 16 shortcuts, you can even select NONE to reduce the size of the Quick menu and make it easier to navigate.

- Press and hold the MENU/OK button to lock the selector keys, the rear Fn button, and the Q button. Press and hold the MENU/OK button again to remove the key lock.

- Press and hold any of the Fn buttons to directly access the configuration menu for that button. This doesn't work with the video recording button (Fn1), which can only be (re-)assigned through the menu.

- To see where the Fn buttons are located and what's assigned to each of them, simply press and hold the DISP/BACK button. In this menu, you can also reassign all Fn buttons.

- To confirm a new menu selection in shooting mode, you can either press the MENU/OK button or half-press the shutter button.

- Half-press the shutter button to switch from playback mode to shooting mode.

- Half-press the shutter button during an ongoing image preview (SET-UP > SCREEN SET-UP > IMAGE DISP.) to immediately cancel the preview and return to the live view display.

- Half-press the shutter button for a few seconds to wake-up the camera from sleep mode.

- In AF-S shooting mode (with Single Point AF), press the rear command dial to zoom into the currently active AF frame.

- In manual focus (MF) mode, you can also press the rear command dial to enlarge the currently selected focus frame. When zoomed-in, you can choose between two magnification levels by turning the command dial.

- Press and hold the rear command dial in MF mode to cycle between the different manual focus assist modes: standard, focus peaking, and digital split image.

- During selection of an AF frame or AF zone, you can press the rear command dial to reset the AF frame or AF zone to their default size. By turning a command dial, you can change the size of the AF frame or zone. Press the DISP/ BACK button to reset the position of the AF frame or AF zone to the center. You can move the AF frame or zone around with the four selector (arrow) keys.

- In playback mode, you can turn the rear command dial to zoom in and out of an image. By pressing the DISP/BACK button, you can always directly return to the standard-size view. During playback, use the front command dial to browse through the images that are on file.

- In playback mode (while viewing an image), press the rear command dial to zoom into a 100% view of the shot. When you are zoomed-in, pressing the dial again returns the camera to its regular view, displaying the full image.

- While displaying a RAW image in playback mode, you can press the Q button to directly access the built-in RAW converter. This function allows you to create new JPEG versions of your image with different settings.

- In playback mode, press the upper selector (arrow up) button to view the first of two information screens that show additional shooting parameters and the position of the focus point. This function is not available when you are using the FAVORITES display mode.

| TIP 30 | Suggested Fn button assignment |
|---|---|

A smart assignment of your X-T10's seven Fn buttons will save you many cumbersome trips to the camera menu. To display and change the assignment of all Fn buttons in one convenient menu, press and hold the DISP/BACK button in shooting mode until the configuration page named FUNCTION (Fn) SETTING appears.

Here are my suggested Fn button assignments:

- **Fn1: PREVIEW PIC. EFFECT.** With this assignment, the video recording button turns into an on/off switch for the Natural Live View. Unlike the standard WYSIWYG display, Natural Live View (NLV) emulates the display of an optical viewfinder with increased dynamic range in shadow areas. Basically, it's more representative of how our human eyes would see a scene. PREVIEW PIC. EFFECT ON is the camera's normal mode with WYSIWYG simulating (almost) all camera settings in the live view display. PREVIEW PIC. EFFECT OFF activates the Natural Live View, which displays flat colors and shows additional shadow dynamic range. The latter is particularly useful for high-contrast scenes with dark shadow parts because it will reveal more shadow detail in the live view, making it easier to compose the scene. Please note that Fn1 operates with a short time delay, meaning you have to press and hold the button for at least a second to get an effect. That's okay; it prevents us from accidently toggling between the WYSIWYG and NLV display modes. Sadly, there's no permanent symbol in the viewfinder that indicates in which of the two modes the camera is operating. However, a message is briefly displayed when you change the display mode from WYSIWYG mode (PREVIEW PIC. EFFECT ON) to NLV mode (PREVIEW PIC. EFFECT OFF) and back.

- **Fn2: AF MODE.** Fujifilm's new autofocus system premiered in the X-T10. Besides offering a choice between AF-S(ingle) and AF-C(ontinuous) with a switch at the front of the camera, there are also three additional AF modes that can be combined with either AF-S or AF-C: SINGLE POINT, ZONE, and WIDE/TRACKING. In order to quickly switch between these modes, it's useful to assign their selection to one of the Fn buttons. Personally, I prefer Fn2 (the front command dial) for this job.

- **Fn3: PHOTOMETRY (or WHITE BALANCE).** Fn3 is my wild card: this is where I put a function that I'm frequently using for a current task. Typically, this is either a shortcut to switch between the three exposure metering modes or a shortcut to access the WHITE BALANCE options.

- **Fn4: ISO.** Since ISO signal amplification is a very important and frequently used setting, it should be accessible via one of the Fn buttons. There's another reason, too: accessing ISO through an Fn button opens a *transparent* menu, so you can immediately see the effect of any ISO change in the live view image. This results in a more intuitive user experience than blindly changing ISO in the Quick menu or shooting menu.

- **Fn5: DYNAMIC RANGE.** Fujifilm cameras offer a very powerful and high-quality DR function to extend the highlight dynamic range of an image, so it's a good idea to keep this function right at your fingertips.

- **Fn6: FOCUS AREA.** Using the lower selector button to move the active focus point or AF zone around the image frame is a camera default setting, so keeping this important function on Fn6 is a no-brainer.

- **Fn7: FACE DETECTION.** Face Detection is another function that should be at your fingertips when it's required, so putting it on Fn7 makes sense, since this particular button is recessed to avoid pressing it by accident.

<table><tr><td>TIP 31</td><td>Always shoot FINE+RAW!</td></tr></table>

The age-old question of whether to shoot RAW or JPEG isn't really adequate for users of X-series cameras like the X-T10. The best option is using both formats by setting SHOOTING MENU > IMAGE QUALITY > FINE+RAW. It doesn't matter if you consider yourself a diehard RAW shooter or a JPEG shooter.

This is how **diehard RAW shooters** benefit from FINE+RAW:

- During external RAW processing, the camera-made JPEG can be used as a (sometimes hard-to-beat) reference image. Often, users struggle to get better results with post-processing programs than they can with the camera's default instant JPEG.

- Checking critical focus is only possible at 100% magnification, which only a high-resolution JPEG can provide. The JPEG that's embedded in the RAW file for preview purposes is too small. Make sure you select one of the three available L (Large) options under SHOOTING MENU > IMAGE SIZE.

- The IMAGE SIZE menu isn't available in RAW-only mode. Different image formats, such as 1:1 or 16:9, are only available in JPEG-only mode or in FINE+RAW mode. Autofocus and exposure metering adapt to the currently selected format (aspect ratio) and deliver more accurate readings when you are shooting with odd formats like 1:1.

No worries, though: the RAW is always recorded in the sensor's native 3:2 format, so you don't lose any image information. Using the built-in RAW converter to generate a JPEG from a RAW file will always result in full-size 3:2 format JPEGs with maximum resolution.

This is how **diehard JPEG shooters** benefit from FINE+RAW:

- Nobody is capable of always setting the *perfect* shooting parameters (exposure, white balance, dynamic range, as well as JPEG parameters such as film simulation, color, sharpness, noise reduction, shadow and highlight contrast, etc.) in advance. FINE+RAW solves this problem by allowing you to change and adjust those settings after the fact, either with the built-in or an external RAW converter. This means you can worry about those JPEG settings later and concentrate on more important factors of your shot, such as focus, framing, and timing.

- Even if you chose the perfect settings in advance, it's possible that you'd like to have more than one version of a shot, such as a color version and a black-and-white version, or versions with different color film simulations. Again, FINE+RAW does the trick because you can use the built-in RAW converter to create (and compare) different JPEG versions of a shot.

- There's always progress in the digital domain. Things that appear impossible today may be a reality in just a few years. It's perfectly feasible that the RAW converters of the future will be able to extract much better image quality from your RAW files than today's cameras and RAW processors. It pays to be prepared by archiving the digital negatives (aka RAW files) of your valuable shots. Storage space is cheap; some of your images may be priceless.

■ Your skills may improve as well! Several months or a few years from now, you may be much more comfortable using post-processing software than you are today. Wouldn't it be sad if you couldn't revisit great shots of the past and process them in a better way? Don't forget: only RAW files contain the complete information of an image. JPEGs are just a processed and compressed subset with limited latitude for post-processing. RAW files feature much better tonality and dynamic range. By the way, using the built-in RAW converter of the X-T10 isn't more complex or complicated than using the camera's JPEG settings in the shooting menu (which should be familiar to you as a JPEG shooter).

As you can see, RAW+FINE is always the best and most flexible choice. However, the one detrimental aspect of using RAW+FINE is that it results in larger amounts of data. This doesn't matter much in practical terms because the X-T10 features a fast processor that can quickly transfer large amounts of data to a memory card. Just make sure to use a fast card like the SanDisk Extreme Pro with 95 MB/s write speed. A card with a capacity of 32 GB can store more than 700 FINE+RAW image pairs.

Let me use this opportunity to address a widespread misconception: RAW files aren't images that you can directly look at. RAWs contain image *data* that still has to be *translated* or *processed* into an actual image, either in-camera or with external software. Every actual digital image (including the live view on the monitor, JPEGs from the camera, or TIFF files from Adobe Lightroom) is the result of such a translation.

A diehard JPEG shooter who doesn't keep RAW files has to settle for only one of the many possible translations of RAW data into an image, and it's highly unlikely that this single JPEG from the camera is the best of all possible versions of the image. Basically, discarding the RAW file turns the X-T10 into an instant camera: you only get one (most likely not the best) image.

<table><tr><td>Pick a suitable **image format**!</td><td>TIP 32</td></tr></table>

The full resolution of the X-T10 (about 16 megapixels) is only available in its native image format (3:2). However, using a different image format (such as 1:1 or 16:9) can still be reasonable. For example, some people prefer to view their images on a 16:9 HD television, while others are fans of the classic (square) medium format look.

No matter what format (aspect ratio) and resolution you choose in SHOOTING MENU > IMAGE SIZE, it will only affect the JPEGs coming from your camera. RAW files are always recorded in full resolution in the native 3:2 sensor format. This means that you can generate new full-size 3:2-format JPEGs with the built-in RAW converter or an external RAW processor, as long as you kept your RAW files.

If you want to compose shots in the 1:1 or 16:9 formats, you should select the desired format in the shooting menu. Here's why:

- The live view in the viewfinder or on the LCD will automatically adjust to the new format, making it easier to compose an image.

- Size and position of the camera's autofocus frames will adapt to the selected image format. This means that even in the highly cropped 1:1 format, all 49 AF frames will still be available when you are using Single Point AF.

- The camera's exposure metering and live histogram are based on what's displayed in the live view. Changing the live view to 16:9 or 1:1 will enhance metering accuracy for the respective format.

| TIP 33 | The magical half-press |
| --- | --- |

A basic rule for successfully using mirrorless cameras like the X-T10 is minimizing the delay between pressing the shutter button and the camera actually taking the image. It's all about not missing the decisive moment due to shutter lag.

It's up to you to anticipate these decisive moments. You should have the shutter button already half-pressed so you're ready to fully depress it to actually take the shot. By half-pressing the shutter button, you are preparing the camera: exposure and autofocus (unless you are using AF-C) will be set and locked, and the lens aperture will move to its working position. The camera is now ready to record an image with minimal shutter lag—all that's left to do is to fully depress the already half-pressed shutter button at the right instant.

## 2.2 MONITOR AND VIEWFINDER

The X-T10 features a large high-resolution electronic viewfinder (EVF) along with an LCD monitor. Both can be used for either image composition or playback.

| TIP 34 | Make use of the **eye sensor!** |
| --- | --- |

Use the VIEW MODE button to activate the built-in eye sensor. The camera will now automatically switch to whichever view (EVF or rear LCD screen) is in use when you are taking or reviewing images (or making changes to the camera menu).

When you are working with a tripod or holding the tilted LCD display close to your body, the eye sensor can get confused. In such cases, use the VIEW MODE button to set the camera to LCD ONLY.

<table><tr><td>Instant review</td><td>TIP 35</td></tr></table>

To instantly review an image right after you have taken it, you can select SET-UP > SCREEN SET-UP > IMAGE DISP. and then set a display period of 0.5 SEC, 1.5 SEC, or CONTINUOUS. The image will always be displayed in the currently active view (LCD or EVF).

You can immediately cancel an image review and continue shooting by half-pressing the shutter button. With the CONTINUOUS option, you can also zoom into the image using the rear command dial. Pressing the rear command dial will directly zoom to the highest available magnification.

In situations that require you to take a series of shots in quick succession, it may be advisable to switch image review off. To do so, select SET-UP > SCREEN SET-UP > IMAGE DISP. > OFF. With image review off, you can still check your latest shot by pressing the playback button.

Please don't forget that the maximum magnification (to check critical focus) is only available when the camera is set to record RAW *and* JPEG files in size L.

<table><tr><td>The **DISP/BACK button** can be tricky!</td><td>TIP 36</td></tr></table>

The DISP/BACK button serves two different purposes:

- As a BACK button, it returns the camera to a higher menu or selection level without saving any changes you may have made in the menu sub-level.

- As a DISPLAY button, it changes the display mode of the currently active view (LCD monitor or EVF).

It's important to remember that changing the display mode only affects the currently active view. For example, in order to change the display mode of the EVF, the EVF must be in use when you press the DISP/BACK button. This means that when you are using the eye sensor, you must actually look through the EVF while you are pressing the DISP/BACK button. If you don't, you will only change the display mode of the LCD monitor.

When the camera is in shooting mode, the EVF and the LCD monitor can use different display modes at the same time.

In playback mode, the EVF and LCD are synced to the same display mode. In this case it doesn't matter which view (EVF or LCD) is active when you change the playback display mode with the DISP/BACK button.

If you select a display with information overlays in shooting mode, you can also choose which elements are supposed to appear in the viewfinder or on the LCD monitor. Select SET-UP > SCREEN SET-UP > DISP. CUSTOM SETTING and then check the items that you want to be displayed. As mentioned before, I recommend to check all items on the list.

| TIP 37 | WYSIWYG – What You See Is What You Get! |
| --- | --- |

The EVF and LCD monitor of the X-T10 operate in WYSIWYG mode: What You See Is What You Get. This means that the viewfinder and monitor are always trying to display a live view image that closely resembles how the resulting JPEG will look. The live view simulates exposure, colors, contrast, and white balance. Plus, when you half-press the shutter, the camera will set the selected working aperture, so the live view will also display a preview of the depth of field.

The live view's exposure simulation is quite helpful because it allows you to recognize exposure errors before you take the picture. Please note that the live histogram is always based on the current live view image.

The live view's WYSIWYG simulation is available in all four of the camera's exposure modes: program AE P, aperture priority A, shutter priority S, and manual exposure mode M.

In manual mode M, you can switch the exposure simulation off by selecting SET-UP > SCREEN SET-UP > PREVIEW EXP. IN MANUAL MODE > OFF. That way, the X-T10 will always display a bright live view image in manual mode, regardless of the chosen exposure parameters (shutter speed, aperture, and ISO). This can be useful in a studio setting with flash photography. For example, you may want to eliminate the surrounding-light component by stopping down the aperture and fully illuminating your subject with flash lights.

Please note that both the live view and the live histogram aren't representing the actual exposure in this mode, so don't forget to switch the exposure simulation back on with SET-UP > SCREEN SET-UP > PREVIEW EXP. IN MANUAL MODE > ON if you want to work with a proper exposure simulation and live histogram in manual mode M.

The live view's exposure simulation is limited in situations with very low light and slow shutter speeds of several seconds. In these cases, the live view and the live histogram may appear darker than the actual result. In such scenarios, you should first take a test shot and review it in playback mode. The detail information display (which you can select with the DISP/BACK button) will show you a playback histogram of the recorded JPEG image. This includes a preview with "blinkies," which indicate blown (overexposed) highlights. Sadly, the playback histogram only shows the picture's luminance (overall brightness distribution), not its three distinct RGB color channels.

<table><tr><td>TIP 38</td><td>Using the **Natural Live View**</td></tr></table>

The so-called Natural Live View is a display mode that disables the WYSIWYG simulation of JPEG settings such as Film Simulation, Highlight Tone, Shadow Tone, or Color. Instead, it will display a live view image with increased shadow dynamic range and with natural colors that are supposed to resemble what our human eye would see when looking through an optical viewfinder. It will also set the live view to Auto white balance and not simulate any custom white balance settings or presets in the live view. However, all current JPEG and white balance settings will still be applied to the *actual image* that's recorded.

To set the camera to Natural Live View mode, select SET-UP > SCREEN SET-UP > PREVIEW PIC. EFFECT > OFF. This setting enables generic looking previews for color, black-and-white, and sepia shooting that do *not* reflect the look of the actual JPEG results. This makes Natural Live View particularly useful to RAW shooters who can use its increased dynamic range to better see what's going on in the shadowed parts of a high-contrast scene while they are trying to compose the shot.

## 2.3 EXPOSING RIGHT

It's not the job of the camera to find and set the right exposure. This is the job of the photographer. That said, the X-T10 features the usual set of AE (auto exposure) modes: aperture priority **A**, shutter priority **S**, and program AE **P**.

- **Aperture priority A** will automatically set a suitable shutter speed to match a preset aperture based on your exposure.

- **Shutter priority** `S` will automatically set a suitable aperture to match a preset shutter speed based on your exposure.

- **Program AE** `P` will automatically set a suitable aperture and shutter speed combination based on your exposure.

- In addition to that, **Auto-ISO** can contribute a suitable ISO setting (within predefined limits). In digital cameras, ISO is the level of signal amplification applied to an image that has been recorded by the camera's sensor. ISO impacts the brightness of the final image.

It is important to understand that these auto exposure (AE) modes (including Auto-ISO) are not responsible for correctly exposing images; exposure is always the responsibility of the photographer. AE modes automatically fill variables (such as the shutter speed in aperture priority `A`) in a way that matches the exposure that has been set by the photographer. Auto exposure will only deliver good results if the photographer is exposing correctly.

EXPOSING CORRECTLY—HOW DOES THIS WORK?
Don't panic! Unlike conventional DSLR cameras, the mirrorless X-T10 makes things easy. Three different metering modes (multi, spot, and average), the WYSIWYG live view, and the live histogram help you find the correct exposure for any given scene. The most important tool is the exposure compensation dial, which allows you to correct the metered exposure up to ±3 EV in convenient steps of 1/3 EV. EV means Exposure Value, and 1 EV is equivalent to one full aperture stop. The correct exposure isn't what the camera is metering; it's what *you* make of the metering by adjusting the exposure compensation dial.

<table><tr><td>**TIP 39**</td><td>Choosing the right **metering method**</td></tr></table>

There are three different metering methods available to measure the amount of light that goes through the lens and hits the image sensor:

- **Average** metering calculates an unweighted average of the total light that hits the entire sensor area.

- **Spot** metering, on the other hand, is merely looking at two percent of the sensor area. The metering area covers about the size of a medium-sized autofocus frame in the center of the image. Alternatively, you can link spot metering to the size and position of the active autofocus frame (in SINGLE POINT AF and MF mode).

- **Multi** or **matrix** metering calculates a weighted average of the total light that hits the sensor. The weight is a result of 256 metering areas (the matrix) that the camera evaluates and compares to typical scenarios. That's why multi metering is considered "smarter" than the two other methods. For example, multi metering is designed to recognize when you are shooting against the sun.

All three metering methods return exposure recommendations based on middle gray. In other words, when you take a picture of a black wall and then a picture of a white wall, the results will look middle gray. This means:

- If you want the black wall to actually look dark black in the resulting image, you have to manually adjust the exposure downward.

- If you want the white wall to actually look bright white in the resulting image, you have to manually adjust the exposure upward.

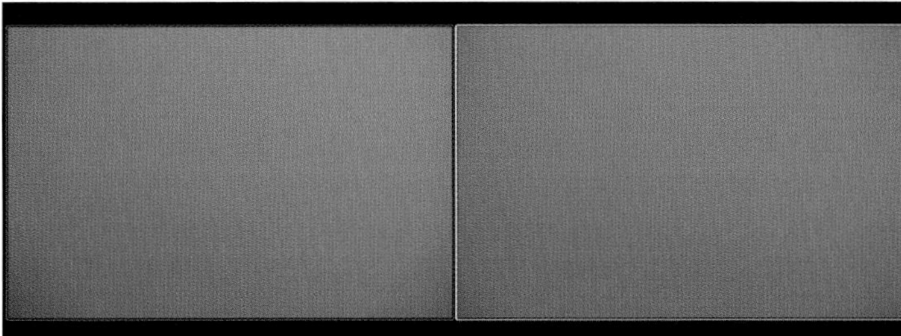

Fig. 22:  This illustration shows a black sheet of paper and a white sheet of paper. Both were photographed with the camera's spot metering without any exposure correction. As you can see, the camera delivered a **middle-gray exposure** in both cases. In order to get an image that reflects the actual brightness of the subject, the metered exposure has to be adjusted.

Since you have read the owner's manual, you know that Fujifilm offers a few recommendations regarding exposure compensation in certain scenarios. For example, the manual recommends a correction of +1 EV when you are shooting in snowfields, or −2/3 EV when you are shooting subjects in spotlight. Instead of these rules, I recommend a more precise and methodical course of action using the live view and the live histogram. To minimize corrective adjustments, it's best to select a metering method that fits the subject or the job at hand:

- **Multi** metering is a general-purpose method. Since it is supposed to be "smarter" than the two other methods, there's a good chance that you won't have to apply any corrective adjustments to the proposed exposure while using this metering method.

- **Average** metering is quite useful for shooting landscapes and will often yield a darker exposure than multi metering, at least when sky and clouds are involved. Average metering is a very neutral metering method that is more likely to stay consistent despite small changes in composition (or framing) than multi metering and spot metering. I recommend average metering if you want to take a series of shots of the same subjects under similar conditions. In such cases, average metering will help you keep the exposure consistent.

- **Spot** metering bases its measurements on one particular spot of the overall image. This means you have to work very precisely to make sure you are metering the appropriate part (spot) of the image. The resulting exposure recommendation will expose this spot with middle-gray brightness. For example, if you spot meter a backlit face against the sun, the metered exposure will display the face with middle-gray brightness (or zone 5 in the famous Ansel Adams zone system). If that's too dark for your taste, you can use the exposure compensation dial to lift the exposure by +1/3 EV or +2/3 EV. On the other hand, if the person has dark skin, you may want to reduce the exposure with a correction in the opposite direction. It's up to you to choose the zone (brightness) of the spot-metered part of the image.

Spot metering is the most powerful and challenging metering method. It's useful when the light is very difficult—too difficult for multi and average metering. Typical examples are isolated bright objects in front of a dark background (and vice versa), such as a musician or an actor on a stage, or strongly backlit subjects. Whenever your exposure has to be spot on, spot metering is your friend.

With that said, it's pretty obvious that spot metering requires you to meter very precisely. Even small changes in where you are pointing the camera can lead to dramatic changes in the metered result. This is why it can be useful to combine spot metering with the camera's AE-L button. AE-L will lock your exposure to prevent it from changing as soon as you alter your composition or your subject starts to move away from your metering spot.

Alternatively, you can use spot metering in manual mode **M**. In this mode, metering doesn't affect the exposure because you are setting all the exposure parameters (shutter speed, aperture, and ISO) manually. Spot metering in manual mode helps you determine the brightness level (zone) of any part of your image for any given exposure. The exposure scale in the viewfinder or LCD tells you exactly how much brighter or darker than middle gray (zone 5) the spot metered object would appear in your shot (±3 EV).

Don't forget to *disable* Auto-ISO in manual mode **M**. If you don't, the camera will still operate in some kind of AE mode (I call it "misomatic"); in this mode, the ISO setting will be the exposure variable that's automatically adjusted.

| Linking spot metering to AF frames | TIP 40 |
|---|---|

Traditionally, spot metering covers the center of the frame with an area that's about as large as a medium-sized (standard) autofocus frame. However, by selecting SHOOTING MENU > INTERLOCK SPOT AE & FOCUS AREA > ON, you can link the spot metering area to the position and size of the active autofocus frame in Single Point AF.

This is a very useful feature if you are using one of the camera's 48 AF frames that *aren't* in the center, since it's likely that your focus area covers the same part of your subject that is also relevant for exposure metering (such as the brightly lit face of a stage actor who is standing in front of a dark background).

If you want to decouple spot metering from the AF area and limit it to the very center of the frame, make sure to select SHOOTING MENU > INTERLOCK SPOT AE & FOCUS AREA > OFF.

Please note that the camera will not interlock spot metering with the focus area if you set the camera to either Zone AF or Wide/Tracking AF. Interlocking only works in concert with Single Point AF and Manual focus (MF) mode.

**TIP 41**  |  Using the **live view and live histogram**

Unlike optical viewfinders in DSLRs, the electronic live view of the X-T10 provides a pretty good simulation of the resulting image. The live preview encompasses colors, contrast, and exposure.

In standard display mode, this WYSIWYG preview is complemented by a live histogram. I strongly recommend using the live histogram because it provides a useful overview of the brightness distribution in your scene. It also helps you identify areas of over- and underexposure in advance, so you can take corrective measures:

- If bars are piling up like a bell curve at the right end of the histogram but cut off mid-peak, parts of your shot will be overexposed with blown highlights. If this affects important parts of your image, you should correct the exposure downward. Alternately, you can expand the camera's dynamic range by selecting DR200% or DR400% in the respective menu.

- If the histogram leans to the left, leaving plenty of space on the right, the shot might end up underexposed. In this case, you can adjust the exposure upward.

The histogram provides a technical representation of the live view simulation. As long as the Natural Live View is turned off, both the live view and the live histogram will reflect the current JPEG settings of the camera (white balance, film simulation, color, highlight and shadow contrast). For example, the VELVIA film simulation will deliver more contrast than PROVIA, and this will be reflected in the live view and the live histogram.

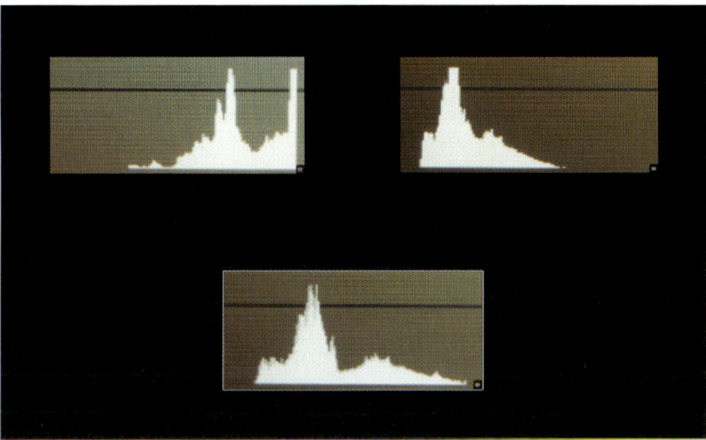

Fig. 23: Different **live histograms** showing overexposure (left), underexposure (right), and a balanced exposure (below)

It's important to note that the live view and live histogram always represent a dynamic range of DR100%, whether the camera's DR is set to AUTO, DR200%, or DR400%. In order to see the effect of an extended DR setting, you have to look at the resulting JPEGs.

| Auto exposure (AE) with modes **P**, **A**, and **S** | TIP 42 |
| --- | --- |

**P** (program AE), **A** (aperture priority), and **S** (shutter priority) are the three auto exposure modes of your X-T10.

A brief reminder:

- **Program AE P** will automatically set a suitable aperture and shutter-speed combination.

- **Aperture priority A** will automatically set a suitable shutter speed to match a preset aperture.

- **Shutter priority S** will automatically set a suitable aperture to match a preset shutter speed.

To take a picture in one of these modes, you can follow these steps:

- Meter the exposure with one of the metering modes: multi, average, or spot.

- After metering, adjust the exposure to taste using the exposure compensation dial. Use the live view and the histogram to determine the best corrections. Remember: it's not the camera that's setting the exposure; it's you. Don't blindly follow what the camera is proposing. Instead, always keep an eye on the live view and the live histogram.

- As soon as you half-press the shutter button, your exposure will be locked as long as you keep the button half-depressed. This means that as long as the shutter button is half-pressed, you can adjust the framing or composition of your shot without changing the exposure.

- Instead of half-pressing the shutter button, you can also use the AE-L button to meter a scene and lock the exposure. You can configure the AE-L button to either lock the exposure as long as you press the AF-L button (SHOOTING MENU > AE/AF LOCK MODE > AE/AF ON WHEN PRESSING), or use the button as a toggle to lock and unlock the exposure (SHOOTING MENU > AE/AF LOCK MODE > AE/AF ON/OFF SWITCH). When the exposure is locked with AE-L, you can still correct it with the exposure compensation dial.

- To take the shot, fully depress the shutter button.

Metering and exposure are two different things. After metering a scene, the photographer sets the actual exposure with the exposure compensation dial:

- **Metering** is performed using either multi, average, or spot metering.

- Use the **exposure compensation dial** to adjust the metering result to taste. Use the information from the live view and live histogram to adjust your settings. Of course, there are many instances where the initial metering is already spot-on, so you won't have to apply any further correction.

- **Expose** the image using one of three AE modes: aperture priority, shutter priority, or program AE.

---

Using **manual exposure** M      TIP 43

---

In manual mode, you manually specify all three exposure parameters: aperture, shutter speed, and ISO amplification. In order for this to work, Auto-ISO has to be turned off. Otherwise, ISO would become an exposure variable that the camera would automatically fill.

For the live view and live histogram to work in manual mode, make sure that SET-UP > SCREEN SET-UP > PREVIEW EXP IN MANUAL MODE > ON is set. I recommend setting the metering to SPOT.

Here's how you can expose in manual mode:

- Select and set an aperture and shutter speed that suits your subject and image idea. Aperture controls the depth of field; shutter speed controls the amount of motion blur in your exposure.

- Next, select an ISO value that will yield the desired brightness in your shot. You can (and should) use the live view and live histogram to find a suitable setting. As usual, try not to blow out important highlights. The live histogram is your friend.

- You can check specific parts of your scene by spot metering them. The exposure scale in the live view screen tells you how much above or below middle gray (zone 5) the spot metered selection will be exposed. This tool helps you ensure that important parts of your image (such as the skin tones of a face) will be exposed exactly like you want them to be.

- Finally, you may want to readjust or fine-tune aperture, shutter speed, and ISO according to your metering. Once everything is set, you can take the shot(s).

> **TIP 44**  Using **aperture priority** **A**

In aperture priority AE, you manually set a specific aperture, and the camera automatically selects a suitable shutter speed based on your chosen exposure (as set with the exposure compensation dial). Which aperture should you select? Let's have quick look at some basics:

- As the aperture gets smaller (the aperture number gets higher), your depth of field (DOF) increases. DOF is the zone in front of and behind the focus plane that appears in perfect focus in your resulting image. In custom display mode, the EVF and LCD offer a focus and DOF bar that displays the focus distance and the calculated depth-of-field zone that surrounds it.

- Fast lenses like the XF56mmF1.2 or the XF35mmF1.4 often exhibit a tight DOF of less than an inch when used wide open, so it's possible, for instance in a portrait shot, for only one of the subject's eyes to be perfectly in focus. If that's the case, you can stop down the lens or change the position of your subject so that both eyes are exactly the same distance to the camera.

- Stopping down a lens beyond f/11 leads to increased diffraction blur across the image area. While the larger depth of field increases the focus zone, maximum detail is reduced. In other words, when you shoot with f/22, there's a good chance that your scene will be in focus from front to back. However, its overall crispness will be lower than it would be at f/8. The Lens Modulation Optimizer (LMO) in your X-T10 can compensate for diffraction blur to a degree, but its effect only extends to JPEGs from the camera, including those created by the built-in RAW converter. External RAW converters don't support the LMO.

- When you shoot wide open or with a high ISO setting, it's possible that the suitable shutter speed is faster than the camera's maximum speed of 1/4000s. If that's the case, the shutter speed will be displayed in red (overexposure warning). You can use shutter speeds beyond 1/4000s by engaging the camera's electronic shutter.

| Using **shutter priority** S | TIP 45 |
| --- | --- |

Shutter priority AE works like aperture priority, except you are manually setting a shutter speed, and the camera will automatically select a suitable aperture value based on your exposure. Shutter priority is only available when you're using native X-mount lenses with electronic contacts. Adapted lenses can only be used with aperture priority or in manual mode.

Setting the right shutter speed is dependent on two factors:

- Motion blur: The faster your subject is moving, the faster your shutter speed has to be in order to avoid shots with motion blur. This doesn't mean that motion blur is always bad. It can be used as a conscious choice to add dynamic punch to your image. In addition to that, panning the camera blurs the background behind a sharp main subject. Motion blur can be a benefit of long exposures—exposure times of several seconds or minutes can smoothen water surfaces, blur cloudy skies, or add star trails.

- Blur due to camera shake: if you don't hold the camera steady when you take a shot, the resulting image can be blurred. The optical image stabilizer (OIS) of the XC and XF zoom lenses can help, or you can put the camera on a tripod or a solid surface and use the self-timer or a remote shutter release to take the shot. A rule of thumb suggests using at least the reciprocal of the (35mm equivalent) focal length as your shutter speed. For example, if you are using a 200mm lens on your X-T10 (and the OIS has been switched off), your minimum shutter speed should be 1/300s, since you have to multiply the focal length with the APS-C crop factor of 1.5. Of course, rules of thumb don't apply to every situation. It really depends on your technique and whether or not you're blessed with steady hands.

If you set a very slow shutter speed or choose a high ISO setting, it's possible that even the smallest aperture opening of your lens will still be too large to avoid overexposure. In this case, the aperture value will be displayed in red.

You can quickly change the shutter speed in full-stop increments using the shutter speed dial. You can also use the front command dial to fine-tune your selection in 1/3 EV intermediate steps. The camera's maximum flash synchronization speed of 1/180s is available on the shutter speed dial.

*Hint: Setting the shutter dial to **T** (Time) allows you to select the **full** range of available shutter speeds (in 1/3 EV steps) by turning the front command dial.*

| TIP 46 | Using **program AE** P **and program shift** |
| --- | --- |

In program AE, the camera will automatically pick a combination of aperture *and* shutter speed settings that correspond to your chosen exposure. This mode can be useful for inexperienced photographers or in situations when you don't have the time to manually adjust the aperture or shutter speed.

In program AE, the slowest possible shutter speed is 4 seconds. When this is not sufficiently slow for the shot you are attempting (in concert with a wide-open aperture), the camera will display a red underexposure warning.

Even in program AE, you can influence shutter speed and aperture to a degree by using program shift. Program shift allows you to select a better combination of aperture and shutter speed than the one originally proposed by the camera's program AE. You can cycle through different combinations of apertures and shutter speeds that all result in the same exposure. Use program shift by turning the command dial. The shifted parameters will be displayed in yellow.

*Important: Program shift is only available when certain conditions are met—it's not available if Dynamic Range is set to AUTO or if a TTL flash unit is in use.*

| Playing it safe with **auto exposure bracketing** | TIP 47 |
| --- | --- |

As you know by now, the automatic exposure (AE) modes **P**, **A**, and **S** are merely responsible for selecting the correct exposure parameters. The exposure itself is the responsibility of the photographer. You can use metering (multi, average, or spot), the live view, and the live histogram to determine the right exposure.

Nobody is perfect! If you want to play it safe, auto exposure bracketing can be a helpful feature. In this mode (DRIVE dial to BKT1 and SHOOTING MENU > BKT/Adv. SETTING > BKT1 SETTING > BKT SELECT > AE BKT), the camera takes a series of three shots in quick succession, each with a different exposure: one shot with normal exposure, one underexposed shot, and one overexposed shot. You can set the under- and overexposure by ±1/3 EV, ±2/3 EV, or ±1 EV.

Exposure bracketing is especially useful with subjects that don't move. After you've taken the shot, you can decide which of the three differently exposed versions you want to keep.

<table><tr><td>TIP 48</td><td>**Long exposures**</td></tr></table>

Long exposures can lead to impressive results. Fireworks, night shots, water surfaces, stars, or clouds: exposure times of several seconds or minutes capture the course of time in a single photograph. Of course, this only works if you put the camera on a tripod or a solid surface.

You have two basic options:

- Set the shutter-speed dial to **T** (Time) and then use the front command dial to set the shutter speed down to 30 seconds. In order to avoid camera shake, use a remote shutter release or the self-timer to take the shot.

- Set the shutter speed dial to **B** (Bulb), then press and hold the shutter as long as you want the camera to expose. The maximum length is 60 minutes. Obviously, it makes sense to use a remote shutter release that can be locked for the duration of the shot.

For good-quality results, make sure to set SHOOTING MENU > LONG EXPOSURE NR > ON. By doing so, the camera will perform a dark-frame subtraction depending on what ISO and exposure time is used. Dark-frame subtraction doubles the effective exposure duration, so be patient.

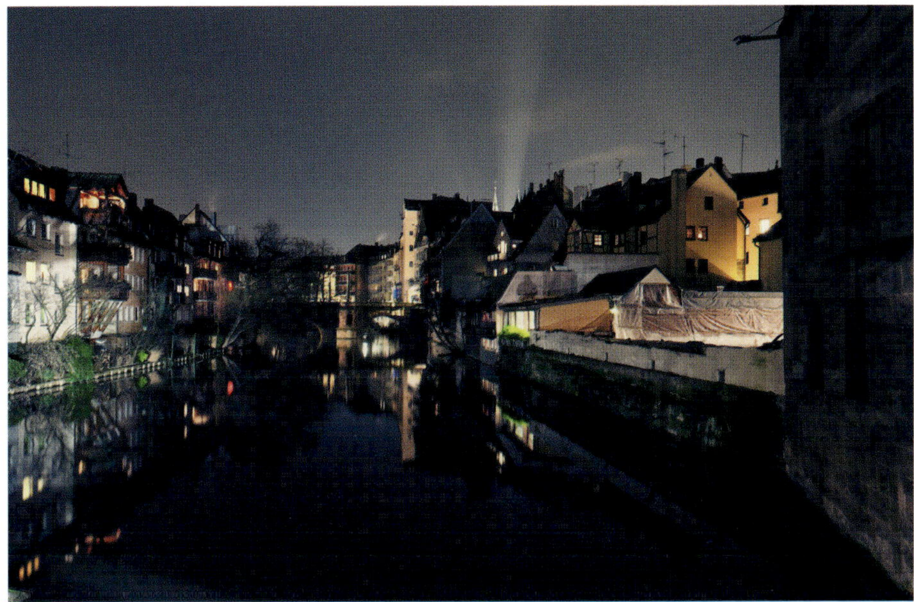

Fig. 24:  Night shot with **30 seconds of exposure** in T mode. Make sure to use a solid tripod and a remote shutter release for these kinds of shots.

| Long exposures in bright daylight | TIP 49 |
| --- | --- |

In order to achieve long exposure times under normal daylight conditions, you can't just stop down the lens—even at f/22, your shutter speed would still be too fast. Besides, diffraction blur is kicking it beyond f/11, so stopping down beyond this point is only recommended when it cannot be avoided.

To realize long shutter speeds in good light, it's best to use a so-called ND filter, or Neutral Density filter. This is a fancy name for a simple gray filter that you can put in front of the lens to block a portion of the light from reaching the sensor.

For example, a filter with an ND 3.0 specification will extend your exposure time by a factor of about 1,000 (or 10 f-stops). This means that by using such a filter, a scene that would normally require a shutter speed of 1/50s at f/11 can be shot at the same aperture with an exposure time of 20 seconds.

However, there's a catch: since your X-T10 is equipped with a rather weak infrared cut filter in front of the sensor, long exposures (typically one minute or longer) in bright daylight should be performed not only with a regular neutral density (ND) filter, but also with a dedicated IR cut filter in front of the lens. This will help you avoid false colors. A few ND filters already include an IR cut filter.

| TIP 50 | ISO settings—what's the deal? |

The meaning of ISO in the digital realm is often misunderstood. Higher ISO settings *don't* increase the sensor's sensitivity. The sensor in your X-T10 is calibrated to its native ISO 200, and this remains the same no matter what ISO you set in the camera.

To be clear, there's no difference between taking a shot with f/5.6 and 1/60s at either ISO 100 or at ISO 25600. In both cases the sensor is exposed to the exact same amount of light (or photons). The amount of light (the real exposure) is solely determined by aperture and shutter speed.

So what exactly is ISO doing? ISO determines the amount of *signal amplification* that's applied to the image recorded by the sensor. ISO 200, the sensor's native setting, is equivalent to the camera's basic calibration. At ISO 400, the signal (or sensor data) is amplified by one aperture stop to brighten the image and increase its exposure. At ISO 800, the amplification amounts to two stops, and so on. At ISO 25600, the additional amplification of the light recorded by the sensor amounts to seven stops. It's not surprising that image quality decreases when ISO amplification increases; noise and artifacts are also amplified along with the actual image data.

The amplification we are talking about means brightening the image by increasing its exposure. If you are familiar with external RAW converters such as Lightroom, you know there's an exposure slider. Moving this slider to the left or right changes the exposure (and hence the ISO) of an image. So the concept of ISO amplification isn't limited to the camera itself—it's part of the entire workflow from exposure via RAW file (digital negative) to the final JPEG or TIFF file (digital print).

If you take a shot with an ISO 800 setting, you're telling the camera to expose the image two stops darker than it would at its base ISO of 200, then amplify (brighten) that image two stops to compensate for the underexposure.

Regarding image quality and ISO, there's a basic rule: lower ISO settings lead to higher-quality results, hence the general recommendation to keep the ISO settings as low as possible. However, we obviously can't shoot with ISO 200 all the time, especially in low-light situations.

There are two basic methods to amplify a digital image:

- **Analog/digital hybrid-amplification** *prior* **to writing the RAW file:** This method applies a mix of analog and digital signal processing to amplify or push the image to the brightness level that corresponds to the ISO setting. The digitized result of this process is then saved as a RAW file.

- **Digital amplification (push)** *after* **writing the RAW file:** This method changes the brightness of an image during RAW processing *after* the RAW file has been written. The metadata (a.k.a. instructions) in the RAW file will tell the RAW converter what to do, or you can simply adjust the brightness (and hence, ISO) by moving your RAW converter's exposure slider. You can also use your X-T10's built-in RAW converter to increase or decrease the exposure of an image after it's been recorded.

Digital amplification during RAW processing is beneficial because it's reversible. If the amplification (exposure) is too strong, you can always take it back. ISO (a.k.a. exposure amplification) is a volatile aspect of the photography process because it can be changed anytime: in-camera, prior to writing the RAW file, or later during RAW processing. Your X-T10 makes use of this flexibility: up to ISO settings of 1600, the camera uses a combination of analog and digital signal amplification, and the result of this process is burned into the RAW file. Higher ISO settings beyond 1600 are realized by digitally pushing the ISO 1600 RAW file during RAW processing.

Here's an example: if you shoot a scene with f/10 and 1/1000s at ISO 1600, and then shoot the same scene again with f/10 and 1/1000s at ISO 6400, the camera will save exactly the same RAW data in both cases. The difference will only be visible in the respective JPEGs, since the ISO 6400 shot will be pushed up two stops during RAW conversion.

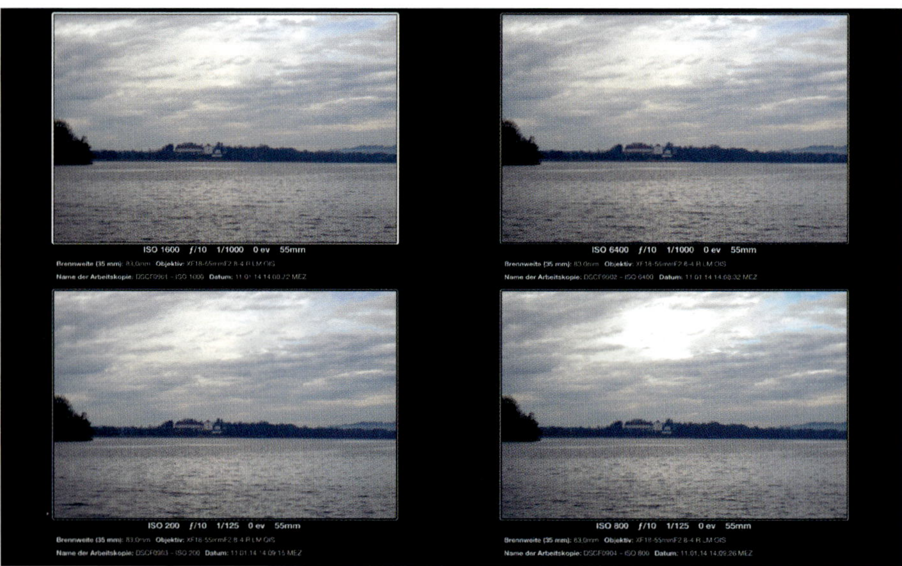


Fig. 25:  The example in the upper row demonstrates how it is possible to turn a shot that was taken at ISO 6400, f/10, and 1/1000s into one that looks exactly like one taken at ISO 1600, f/10, and 1/1000s. All we have to do is pull the exposure slider in our RAW conversion software two stops to the left. There's no loss of quality or dynamic range. This works because any ISO amplification beyond ISO 1600 is applied during RAW conversion and hence, not burned into the RAW file. It is fully reversible.

The example in the lower row shows that this trick doesn't work with ISO 200 and ISO 800, because ISO 800 is already amplified in-camera and the (overexposed) result is irreversibly burned into the RAW file. In this case, bright highlights in the clouds were lost in the ISO 800 shot and could not be recovered by moving the exposure slider in the RAW conversion software two stops to the left.

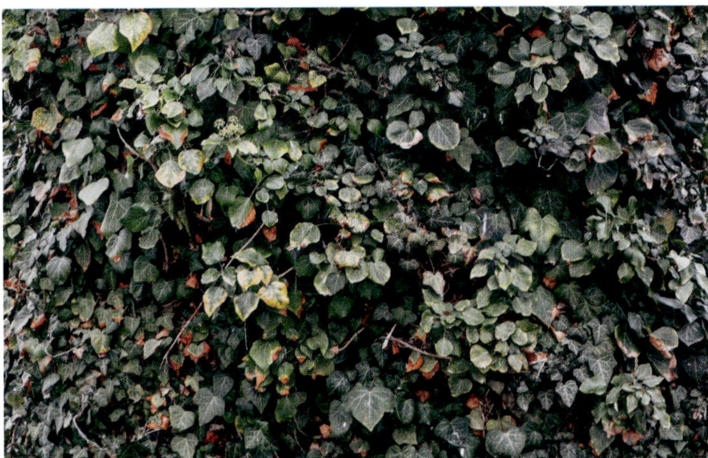

Fig. 26: **ISOless sensor (1):** This shot was taken at ISO 800, with classic analog/digital in-camera amplification from base-ISO 200 to ISO 800. The ISO 800 result was then burned into the RAW file.

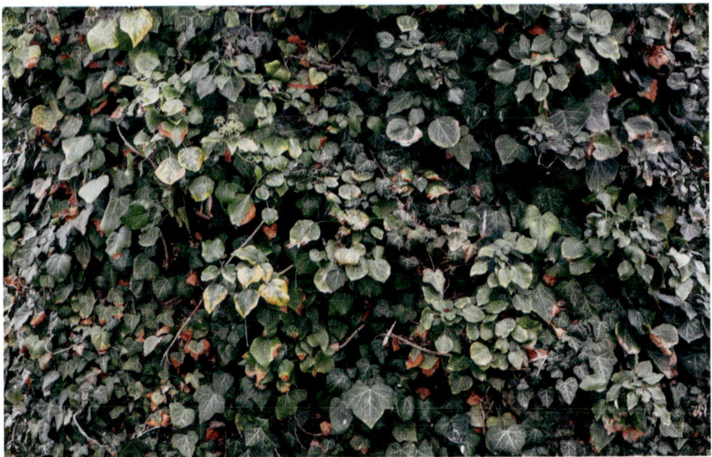

Fig. 27: **ISOless sensor (2):** This shot was also taken at ISO 800. However, the amplification from ISO 200 to ISO 800 took place digitally during RAW conversion. You won't be able to see any quality difference between the two shots in this book, so I invite you to take a look at full-size samples that are uploaded to Flickr. You can access the sample album here: https://www.flickr.com/gp/25805910@N05/20L4L8. Also note that since the X-E2, X-T1, and X-T10 share the same sensor and processor (and hence the same image quality), I have interchanged samples from these cameras in this book.

The sensor in your X-T10 is a so-called an ISOless sensor. This means that there's no relevant quality difference between conventional signal amplification prior to writing a RAW file and digital amplification later during RAW conversion. This is great, because it allows you to digitally increase the ISO (a.k.a. brightness/exposure) of your shots during RAW processing, either in-camera or with external software such as Lightroom. Pushing the exposure up later in Lightroom won't look any different than choosing a higher ISO setting when you take the shot.

| TIP 51 | What you should know about **extended ISO** |

You will probably have noticed that in addition to the standard ISO settings (ISO 200 to ISO 6400), your X-T10 offers four additional settings that are only available when the camera is in JPEG mode (not recording RAW files): L (100), H (12800), H (25600), and H (51200).

- **H means High:** In these modes, a RAW file that has been saved with ISO 1600 will be digitally pushed three stops to ISO 12800, or four stops to ISO 25600. The RAW file is then deleted. This results in correctly exposed JPEG files with ISO 12800 or ISO 25600. This enormous amplification leads to a visible decrease in quality. This is why these extended ISO settings should only be used in emergencies.

- **L means LOW:** In this mode, an ISO 200 RAW that has been overexposed by one stop is pulled down one stop during RAW conversion, resulting in an ISO 100 JPEG. A digital pull is the direct opposite of a digital push operation: it decreases the exposure of the resulting image. Once the JPEG has been created, the (overexposed) RAW file is deleted. The ISO 100 JPEG contains one stop *less* dynamic range than a normal ISO 200 JPEG. Hence, ISO 100 is just another emergency mode, because bright image areas can easily be blown out.

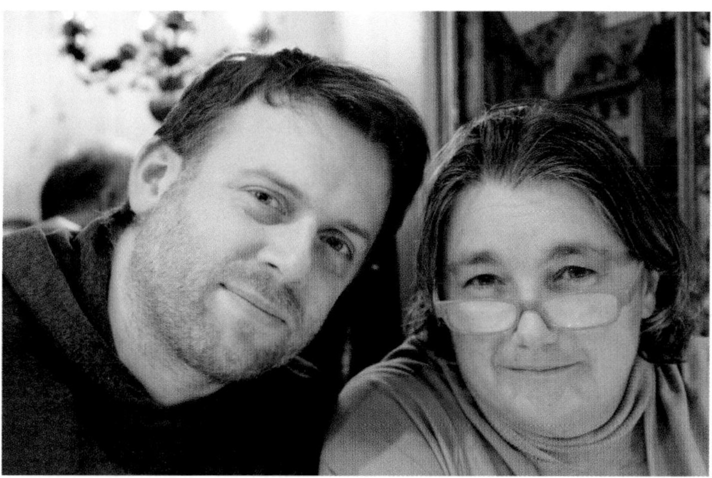

Fig. 28: Instead of using high extended ISO settings and going without RAW files, you can just as well underexpose RAWs with lower ISO settings and push the result later in the built-in or an external RAW converter. This example was taken in very low light with an ISO 5000 setting and then pushed 1 EV to ISO 10000 in the camera's internal RAW converter.

As a RAW or FINE+RAW user, you can create extended ISO modes yourself:

- For ISO 12800 or 25600, you can shoot at ISO 6400 and dial in an exposure compensation of −1 EV (for ISO 12800) or −2 EV (for ISO 25600) with the camera's exposure compensation dial. This results in underexposed RAW files that you can later push one or two stops with the built-in or an external RAW converter.

- Conversely, you can simulate ISO 100 in RAW mode by shooting at ISO 200 and dialing in an exposure compensation of +1 EV. This results in an overexposed RAW file that you can later pull down by one stop with the built-in or an external RAW converter. Like its extended ISO L cousin, this trick will result in losing one stop of dynamic range.

The drawback of this do-it-yourself method is that the live view will appear either too dark or too bright due to the initial under- and overexposure of the RAW files. After all, the correct exposure is only achieved later during a manual RAW conversion that includes pushing or pulling the result to the desired exposure level.

To read more about extended ISO in my *X-Pert Corner* blog, go to the following link: www.fujirumors.com/how-to-use-extended-iso/.

<table><tr><td>TIP 52</td><td>Stay away from ISO 51200!</td></tr></table>

The X-T10 also offers ISO 51200 as an extended ISO setting. In practical terms, ISO 51200 rarely offers sufficient image quality for serious applications, so my recommendation is to not use it. It's an extended ISO setting, which forces the camera to operate in JPEG-only mode, so you can't get a RAW file of your shots.

As a better alternative, I recommend underexposing the images at ISO 6400 in FINE+RAW mode. Then use an external RAW converter to further push them up to 3 stops.

<table><tr><td>TIP 53</td><td>Auto-ISO and minimum shutter speed</td></tr></table>

You can automate the task of selecting the best (or lowest) ISO setting possible for any given shooting situation. Auto-ISO is an option with three configurable presets (AUTO1, AUTO2, AUTO3) in the ISO menu (SHOOTING MENU > ISO):

- DEFAULT SENSITIVITY: This is the lower ISO limit. The camera will always try to use this ISO setting as long as the other parameters allow it.

- MAX. SENSITIVITY: This is the upper ISO limit. The camera's Auto-ISO will never go beyond this point.

■ MIN. SHUTTER SPEED: Auto-ISO will automatically increase the ISO setting (up to the MAX. SENSITIVITY threshold) when the minimum shutter speed cannot be realized.

Obviously, MIN. SHUTTER SPEED is only relevant in auto exposure (AE) modes **A** and **P**, because the shutter speed is set manually in modes **M** and **S**. Auto-ISO makes sure that within the lower and the upper ISO limits, the camera will always use a shutter speed that is at least as fast as the set minimal shutter speed.

Here's an example: let's say you are shooting in mode **A** (aperture priority) in bright light conditions using f/5.6. Auto-ISO is set to ISO 200 as the lower limit and ISO 6400 as the upper limit. You have set 1/125s as your minimum shutter speed, because you want to avoid motion blur while taking pictures of people walking in the street.

As long as the light is bright, there is no problem. The camera will use ISO 200 with shutter speeds at least as fast as 1/125s. However, as the sun sets, it becomes impossible to successfully use 1/125s at f/5.6 and ISO 200, so Auto-ISO will increase the ISO to ensure that the shutter speed doesn't drop below 1/125s. This continues as the light conditions deteriorate until Auto-ISO reaches the upper ISO limit (in our case, ISO 6400). What now? Since the camera can't increase the ISO any further, it will start to reduce the shutter speed to values slower than 1/125s in order to still ensure a correct exposure.

In mode **S** (shutter priority), the photographer sets the shutter speed. In this mode, Auto-ISO will increase the ISO setting only when the aperture is already wide open. This can be a problem with fast lenses like the XF56mmF1.2, XF35mmF1.4, or XF23mmF1.4. When shot wide open, the depth of field of these lenses is quite limited (to say the least). That's why Auto-ISO is better used in modes **P** or **A**, at least in concert with fast lenses.

You can read more about Auto-ISO in my *X-Pert Corner* column at the following website: www.fujirumors.com/using-auto-iso/.

<table><tr><td>TIP 54</td><td>Auto-ISO in manual mode M : the "misomatic"</td></tr></table>

**M**anual mode in concert with Auto-**ISO** turns into another auto**MATIC** exposure mode: the so-called "**misomatic.**" In this mode, you preselect the aperture and shutter speed, and the camera automatically selects a suitable ISO setting that matches the exposure that has been determined by the currently active metering mode (multi, average, or spot).

To be useful in a misomatic application, Auto-ISO should be able to use the full ISO bandwidth, so you should configure it with a lower limit of ISO 200 and an upper limit of ISO 6400.

You have full manual control over aperture (depth of field) and shutter speed (motion blur and camera shake). You can tailor shutter speed and aperture to the requirements of the task at hand; there will be no surprises. At the same time, you still enjoy the comfort of automatic exposure (AE).

Misomatic also allows you to adjust the camera-metered exposure with the exposure compensation dial. For this to be effective, it's even more important to set the Auto-ISO DEFAULT SENSITIVITY to 200 and MAX. SENSITIVITY to 6400.

If you don't want to spend time with exposure compensation while you are in misomatic mode, you can use Fuji's DR function as a workaround by selecting at least DR200% in concert with the misomatic. This setting will give you at least one stop of extra latitude for after-the-fact exposure corrections with the internal or an external RAW converter. Simply use the PUSH or PULL commands of the internal RAW converter, or move the exposure slider of your external RAW processing software.

Don't forget: ISO is just a (mostly digital) amplification of the image signal. Using the misomatic, the amount of light that reaches the sensor is solely determined by your manual aperture and shutter speed settings. It always stays the same, regardless of the automatic ISO setting chosen by the camera. In misomatic mode, the only exposure variable is the amount of signal amplification (a.k.a. ISO), and with an ISOless sensor, this variable can also be adjusted later during RAW conversion. In this context, choosing DR200% ensures that there's ample leeway for after-the-fact exposure corrections of at least ±1 EV.

| ISO-Bracketing: it's just a gimmick! | TIP 55 |
| --- | --- |

ISO bracketing (DRIVE dial to BKT1 and SHOOTING MENU > BKT/Adv. SETTING > BKT1 SETTING > BKT SELECT > ISO BKT) is only available in JPEG mode, so the camera won't keep RAW files. It's just a gimmick: the camera takes a single exposure with the selected ISO setting, then creates two additional JPEGs with different ISO settings, one higher and one lower than the original setting.

ISO bracketing is just a digital push and pull operation on the intermediate RAW file (which is deleted after all three JPEGs have been generated). You could achieve the same result by shooting a single pic in FINE+RAW mode and then using the camera's built-in RAW converter to generate a second JPEG with the PULL command, and a third one with the PUSH command.

A better alternative to ISO bracketing is AE BKT. This option actually takes three different exposures and keeps the corresponding RAW files.

<table><tr><td>**TIP 56**</td><td>**Extending the dynamic range**</td></tr></table>

If the dynamic range of a subject is larger than the dynamic range of the camera's sensor and image processing, one of the following phenomena occurs:

- The highlights of the image are blown out or appear too bright (overexposed).

- Midtones appear too dark (underexposed) and shadows are blocked.

In both cases, the shot's exposure is imbalanced. Sadly, it's very difficult (if not impossible) to restore blown highlights. It's much easier to lift underexposed midtones and blocked shadows. This procedure is called tone mapping. Certain tonal values of the original exposure are reassigned and changed, either by employing a tone curve or by using a more complex mathematical procedure known as adaptive tone mapping.

In order to record the full tonal range of a high-contrast subject, it's best to expose the image in a way that preserves the color and texture of the bright parts of the photo. Of course, doing so can lead to an image with underexposed midtones and blocked shadows that need further processing in order to look natural and realistic. You can correct these issues with most external RAW converters.

While every RAW converter is different, most programs offer functions to selectively change the exposure of a shot. For example, you can change the overall exposure with the exposure slider, and you can restore blown highlights with a highlight restoration slider. Most converters also offer sliders that only target shadow tones.

The DR function of the X-T10 can help you automate this tone-mapping procedure. It works in two stages:

- The RAW file is exposed one (DR200%) or two (DR400%) stops darker in order to preserve bright highlights of a scene.

- During the following RAW conversion in the camera, the darkened shadows and midtones are digitally amplified by one (DR200%) or two (DR400%) stops to restore their natural brightness, while the (already correctly exposed) highlights are mostly left alone.

The resulting JPEG from the camera has undergone a selective exposure correction. The DR function restores the shadows and midtones of a shot that was initially exposed one or two stops darker to preserve the highlights of the scene. Looking at the resulting JPEGs, this leads to an effective gain in dynamic range (DR): one additional stop of highlight DR at DR200%, and two stops of additional highlight DR at DR400%.

In DR-Auto mode, the camera will automatically select a suitable DR setting. Please note that in this mode, the X-T10 will choose either DR100% (no highlight DR expansion) or DR200% (one stop highlight DR expansion). DR400% (two stops highlight DR expansion) is only available when it is manually selected.

You can change the DR settings of your camera in the Quick menu or by selecting SHOOTING MENU > DYNAMIC RANGE and then either AUTO, DR100%, DR200%, or DR400%.

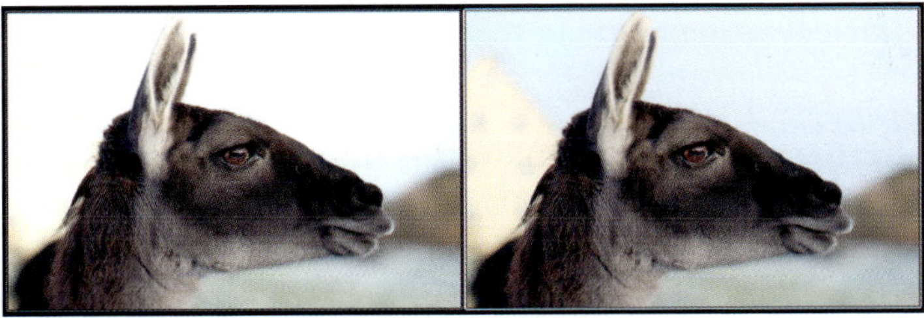

Fig. 29: These examples show the same shot with DR100% (left) and DR400% (right). At DR100%, the dark llama (our main subject) is correctly exposed, but the much brighter colors in the background are almost completely blown because they were outside of the camera's dynamic range. In the DR400% version of the shot, the exposure (brightness) of the llama didn't change. However, the bright background is now perfectly colored and textured.

| TIP 57 | Extending the dynamic range for RAW shooters |

RAW shooters typically set the camera to DR100% and perform the tone mapping of their shots later during RAW processing. DR100% provides a realistic live view and live histogram (WYSIWYG) since the current firmware of the X-T10 cannot simulate the JPEG results of extended DR settings (DR200% or DR400%).

The typical strategy of a RAW shooter is to expose toward the highlights of a high-contrast scene, making sure that there's sufficient color texture in the bright parts of the shot. This can result in an image with dark midtones and blocked shadows. However, while blown highlights are hard to restore, blocked shadows can be lifted (pushed). This can be done in almost any external RAW conversion software to get balanced results from scenes with a very high dynamic range.

Here's what to do:

- Use the live view and live histogram to adjust the exposure in a way that ensures that the important highlights of your scene don't blow. This will preserve the highlights, but it may also lead to darkened midtones and blocked shadows that you have to deal with later during the RAW conversion of your shot.

- Enhance darkened shadows and midtones by selectively lifting their exposure in your RAW conversion software. For example, you could first lift the overall exposure and then restore the highlights with a highlight-restoration slider, or you could only lift the shadow tones with a shadow-tone slider. You can also combine both methods; many RAW converters are quite flexible and offer several sliders to selectively change the exposure. Lightroom and Adobe Camera RAW (ACR), for example, feature five different controls (exposure, whites, blacks, shadows, and

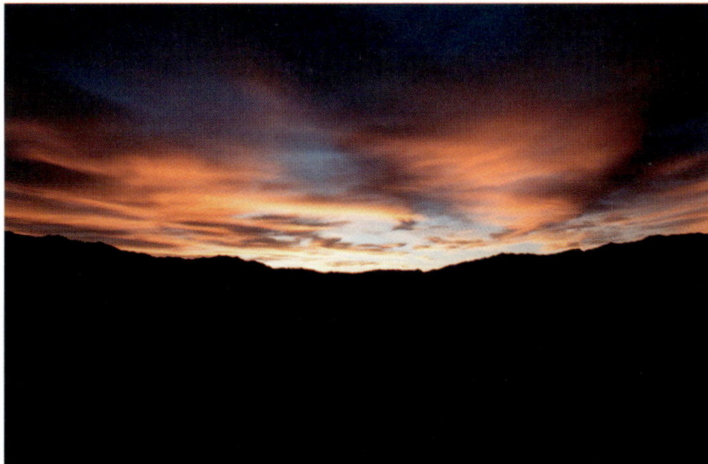

Fig. 30: This is how an image that has been exposed to the highlights looks. The morning sky over Zabriskie Point is perfectly exposed, but this means that the unlit foreground is literally left in the dark. If that's what you want, great! If not, you have to apply some tone mapping to the RAW file.

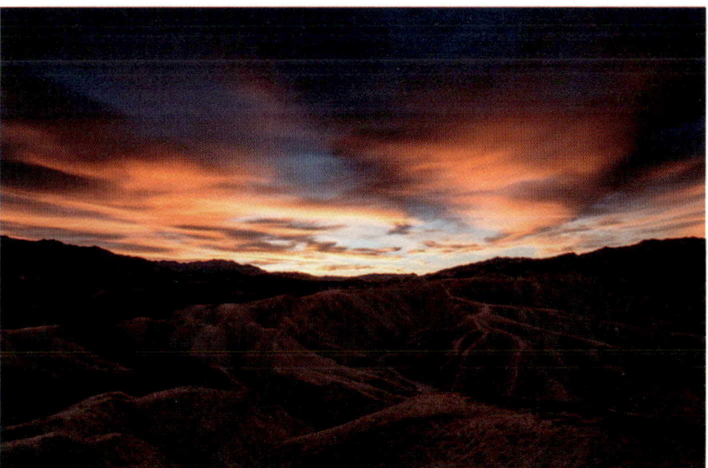

Fig. 31: Here's how the same image looks after some tone mapping in Adobe Lightroom. The dark shadow regions have been lifted, revealing plenty of detail where the previous image only displayed a dark patch. This method is also known as applying adaptive ISO, because different parts of the image received a different degree of exposure push. While the shadows were pushed up (ISO increase), the highlights mostly remained as they were.

highlights) to perform this task. Whenever you change an exposure slider, you are effectively changing the ISO of any part of the image that is affected by this slider. However, in the digital domain of the RAW conversion stage, nothing is lost and everything is fully reversible. *Selectively* changing the exposure of an image is known as tone mapping.

| TIP 58 | JPEG settings for RAW shooters |
| --- | --- |

The previous tip explained the procedure to capture, compress, and later decompress scenes with high dynamic range. Since our exposure relies on the live view and the live histogram, it's useful to find camera settings that force the live histogram and live view to display as much dynamic range as possible. After all, we are shooting RAW and aren't really interested in the JPEGs from the camera, so we want the live view and live histogram to closely represent the data that will be recorded in the RAW files. This goal can be achieved by choosing JPEG parameters that display as much dynamic range as possible:

- Set FILM SIMULATION to PRO NEG. STD. This setting results in JPEGs with less contrast than the other film simulation modes.

- Set HIGHLIGHT TONE (–2) SOFT. This setting reduces the highlight contrast of the JPEG—in the live view and in the live histogram.

- Set SHADOW TONE (–2) SOFT. This setting reduces the shadow contrast of the JPEG in both the live view and the live histogram.

The above JPEG settings give you a live view and live histogram with maximum dynamic range. JPEGs that are generated with these settings may look flat, but we don't care because we don't want to keep them anyway. We are only interested in the RAW file, which isn't affected by JPEG settings at all. However, the live view and live histogram are fully affected, and a flat image live view with a correspondingly flat image live histogram is exactly what we want in order to better fine-tune our exposure to preserve highlights.

You can save these JPEG settings in a custom profile (C1 to C7) so you can quickly retrieve them to set your X-T10 to RAW shooter mode.

*Hint: An alternative to these JPEG settings is using the camera's Natural Live View mode. To enable Natural Live View, select SET-UP > SCREEN SET-UP > PREVIEW PIC. EFFECT > OFF. Natural Live View lifts the shadows and decreases the overall contrast of the live view image. Of course, the Natural Live View doesn't only affect the appearance of the live view image, but also the live histogram, which makes it a reasonable choice for RAW shooters.*

| Extending the dynamic range for JPEG shooters | TIP 59 |
| --- | --- |

If you prefer to work with JPEGs from the X-T10 (or want to shoot both RAW and JPEG), you can use the camera's powerful DR function to capture scenes with high dynamic range. As you know, the DR function employs a two-stage process: reducing the exposure to capture critical highlights, and then lifting dark shadows and midtones to restore their brightness (exposure) back to realistic-looking levels.

If you want to use this function without giving it much thought, you can simply set the camera to DR-Auto, or manually set DR200% or DR400% when you take pictures of high-contrast scenes. Remember that DR200% requires a minimum ISO setting of 400, while DR400% requires a minimum ISO setting of 800, because the shadows in your scene will eventually be amplified by one (DR200%) or two (DR400%) stops. It's best to set the camera to Auto-ISO, allowing it to pick a suitable ISO setting that corresponds with whatever DR setting you or the camera (in DR-Auto mode) may choose.

But what if we don't want to just *guess* what DR setting is optimal for any given scene? Can't we use the camera's metering to determine *exactly* how much DR expansion is required? Yes, we can!

Here's how:

■ To begin with, let's expose toward the critical highlights of a scene, just like a RAW shooter would do. This will often require you to turn the exposure compensation dial in the negative direction until the live view and live histogram display the scene without blown highlights.

■ Next, turn the exposure compensation dial in the opposite (positive) direction until the shadows and midtones are displayed as bright as you want them to appear in the final image. Here's the important part: when you turn the exposure compensation dial up again, count the number of clicks it takes to reach the target brightness of your scene. One, two, or three clicks mean you should set the camera to DR200% for one stop of additional highlight dynamic range. More than three clicks means you should use DR400%. More than six clicks means that highlights may be blown even when you set DR400%, so you might want to avoid overcompensating beyond six clicks. As you know, each click of the exposure compensation dial equals 1/3 EV (or a third of a stop).

*Important: Don't use the Natural Live View in concert with the DR function. Make sure that SET-UP > SCREEN SET-UP > PREVIEW PIC. EFFECT > ON is set.*

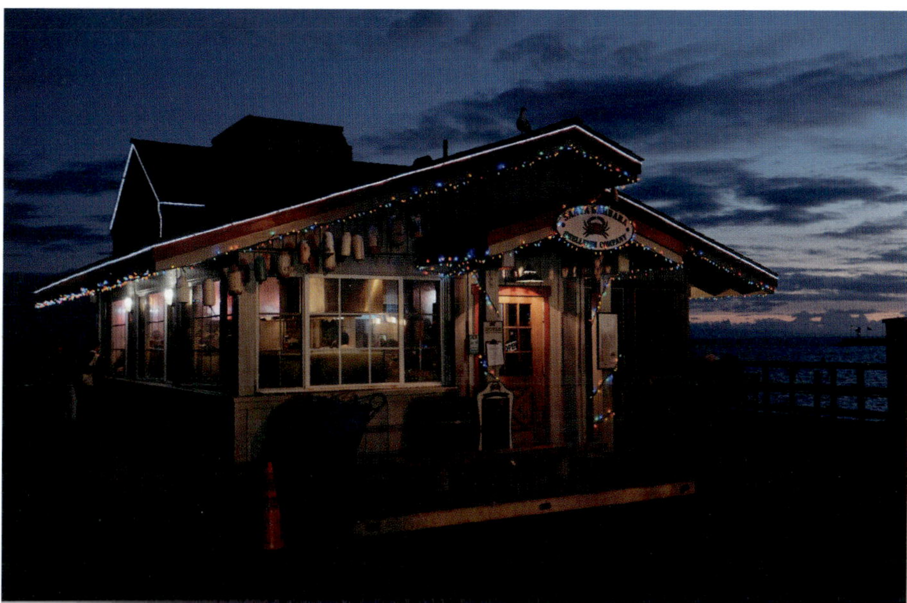

Fig. 32: **Night scenes** with bright lights and high contrast can benefit from a fixed DR400% setting in order to preserve color and texture in the highlights (Classic Chrome, DR400%)

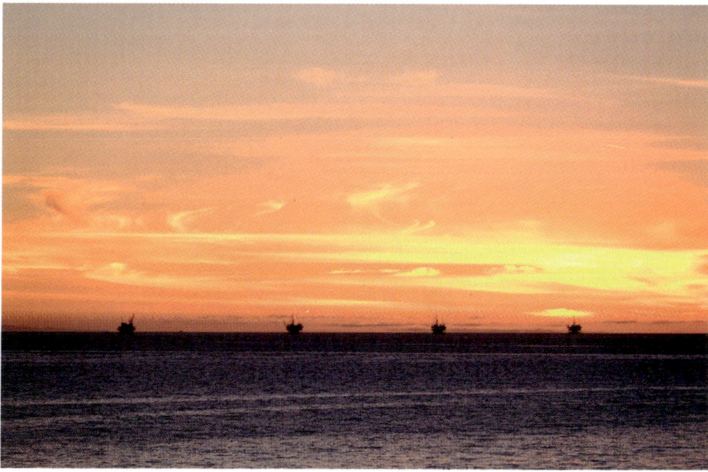

Fig. 33: On the other hand, there are instances where you may want to concentrate on the bright parts of a high-contrast scene. In such cases, a fixed DR100% setting is in order while you are exposing to the highlights (Velvia, DR100%).

The two above examples illustrate that DR-Auto is not a "smart" setting; it cannot predict what the photographer has in mind. In both cases, DR-Auto would have picked DR200%—definitely not an optimal setting in either case.

| TIP 60 | Using the DR function for high-key and portrait photography |

High-key photography delivers images with tones that mostly occupy the right half of the histogram. High-key images can be achieved by lighting a scene brightly and uniformly, with little differences in contrast, then overexposing the scene by one or two stops. This results in images with a bright, clean, and joyful look. This is why high-key is often used for product shots, portraits, and advertising.

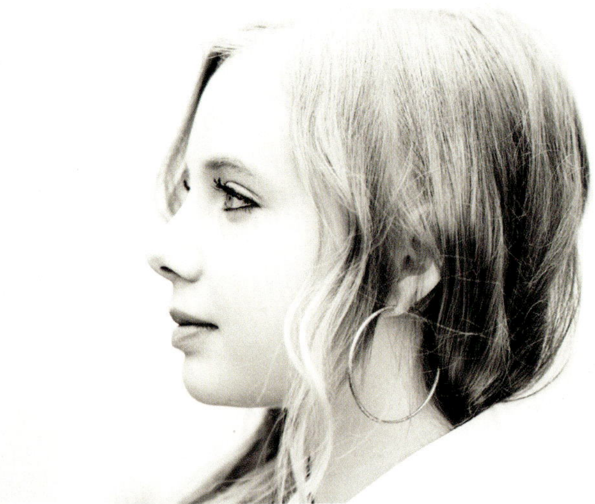

Fig. 34: I took this **high-key sample** under an overcast sky with soft, uniform natural lighting and by placing the model in front of a bright wall. Thanks to the resulting low contrast, the scene could be shot with a bright exposure at ISO 200 and DR100% without blowing critical highlights.

Normally, high-key photographs require suitable low-contrast lighting. If the contrast is too big, a bright exposure of the darker tones would lead to blown highlights.

Remember that to be suitable for high-key, most of your scene has to fit into the right half of the histogram. If that's not the case, there are two options: you can either reduce the contrast of the scene by applying fill light (like installing a flash setup), or you can apply appropriate tone mapping (pushing the shadows and midtones while protecting the highlights) during RAW conversion.

Thanks to the DR function, the second option is also available in-camera. This means that you can generate JPEGs with a high-key look directly in your X-T10.

Here's how:

- Set the camera to manual exposure mode **M** and turn off Auto-ISO, so aperture, shutter speed, and ISO can be set manually. Also, make sure to set the dynamic range to DR100% in the shooting menu or Quick menu.

- Expose the scene as usual to protect critical highlights that you do not want to blow. The live view and live histogram are your friends. Set aperture, shutter speed, and ISO accordingly and take a test shot to be sure that the scene is exposed as brightly as possible without blowing critical highlights.

- Now double your ISO setting (for example, from ISO 200 to ISO 400) and change the dynamic range setting from DR100% to DR200%. Don't change your aperture and shutter speed, though!

- In the live view and live histogram, your scene is now looking overexposed with blown highlights. Don't worry, just ignore it. Instead, take another shot with these new settings and inspect the resulting high-key JPEG in your camera's playback mode.

As far as the RAW data is concerned, it makes no difference whether you shoot the very same scene with ISO 200, DR100%, f/5.6, and 1/1000s or with ISO 400, DR200%, f/5.6, and 1/1000s. Even ISO 800, DR400%, f/5.6, and 1/1000s would result in exactly the same RAW data all over again. However, you will see a huge difference in the corresponding straight-out-of-camera JPEGs, as shadows and mid-tones will appear increasingly bright (high-key), while the brightest highlights are protected and not blown: this is the X-T10's built-in tone mapping at work.

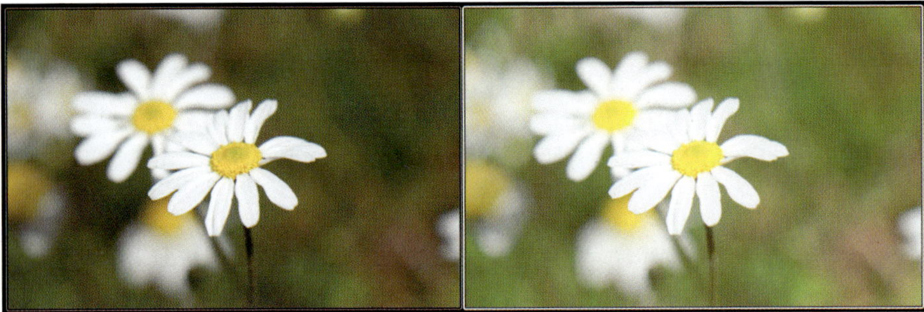

Fig. 35: **Turning the DR function into a virtual high-key studio:** The example on the left illustrates a regular exposure of a flower at ISO 200, DR100%, f/5.6, and 1/1000s. The exposure was designed to protect the structure of the white petals. The example on the right is the same scene shot at ISO 400, DR200%, f/5.6, and 1/1000s. This means that while the RAW data remains the same, only the JPEG from the ISO 400 / DR200% version delivers the desired high-key look while the structure of the petals remains intact. Doubling ISO and DR settings in concert (leaving all other exposure parameters untouched) moved the histogram of the shot to the right, but without blowing bright highlights. Instead of cutting them off, the tonality of the bright highlights is compressed. You can fine-tune such results with the camera's built-in RAW converter, for example, by reducing the highlight contrast (HIGHLIGHT TONE settings). Additionally, you can revert a high-key shot that was taken (for example) at ISO 400 / DR200% into a regular ISO 200 / DR100% JPEG by reprocessing the RAW image in the built-in RAW converter using PULL −1 EV and DR100% settings.

The tone mapping and tonality compression demonstrated in figure 36 can also be used to improve portraits by reducing contrast and harsh shadows in faces that are illuminated by a single light source (like the sun). With our high-key technique, dark eyes and shadows under the nose can be lifted without blowing the bright parts of the skin. At the same time, the tone mapping and highlight tone compression makes skin blemishes almost disappear.

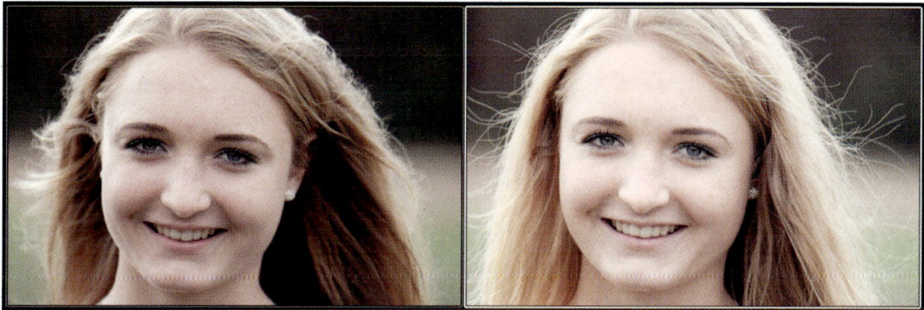

Fig. 36: **Using virtual high-key in a portrait:** The image on the left shows our demo scene at ISO 200, DR100%, f/4, and 1/250s. As usual, I exposed to the brightest parts of the image that I wanted to protect from blowing. Sadly, this resulted in rather dark eyes. The example on the right shows the same scene, but shot with ISO 400, DR200%, f/4, and 1/250s. As you know by now, this makes no difference to the RAW data, but changes the tone mapping of the JPEG engine. With our high-key settings, the eyes and shadows now appear significantly brighter and skin blemishes are obscured. To fine-tune this shot, I reprocessed the ISO 400 high-key version in the built-in RAW converter using PULL −1/3 EV.

| | |
|---|---|
| Creating **HDR images** with the X-T10 | TIP 61 |

A popular method of capturing high-contrast scenes is HDR photography. HDR means High Dynamic Range: multiple images of the scene are taken at different exposure levels and then merged into a single image with extended dynamic range. The latter can be facilitated with specialized software, such as HDR Efex Pro by NIK/Google or Photomatix Pro by HDRsoft.

Typically, HDR requires a minimum of three different exposures of a scene, but some photographers don't stop there. They take five, seven, or even nine different exposures, each separated from the other by (usually) one stop or EV (exposure value).

Here's a procedure that you can use to quickly generate nine different exposures of a scene:

- Put the X-T10 on a tripod or a similar device. If your lens features an OIS, make sure to turn it off.

- Connect a remote shutter release or set the self-timer to 2 seconds to avoid camera shake.

- Set the camera to aperture priority **A**.

- Choose a low ISO setting (such as 200). Don't use ISO 100, though!

- Deactivate any DR expansion by setting the dynamic range to DR100%.

- Select a suitable aperture for your shot and scene and use manual focus. This ensures that all nine images will be focused exactly the same. If you like, you can also use adapted manual focus lenses.

- Set the DRIVE dial to BKT1 and select AE BKT with a variation of ±1 in the bracketing menu to activate the camera's auto exposure bracketing with a variation of ±1 EV.

- Select either MULTI or AVERAGE exposure metering.

Having prepared the camera for HDR, you can now follow these steps to capture the actual images:

- Set the exposure compensation dial to neutral (0) and press the shutter release. Make sure to either use a remote shutter release or the self-timer. The camera will now record the first three shots of the scene, with exposure levels of 0 EV, −1 EV, and +1 EV.

- Set the exposure compensation dial to −3 EV and press the shutter release. The camera is now recording three more images that deviate −4 EV, −3 EV, and −2 EV from the original exposure.

- Finally, set the exposure compensation dial to +3 EV. After releasing the shutter, you'll get three more exposures, this time with +2 EV, +3 EV, and +4 EV.

This procedure results in nine different exposures with an additional dynamic range of ±4 EV that you can merge using the HDR software of your choice.

Please note that the slowest shutter speed in all AE modes is 30 seconds, so your basic exposure (with 0 EV correction) should not be longer than 2 seconds. If you require shots that exceed 30 seconds of exposure time, it's better to use manual mode **M** in concert with the Bulb (B) setting of the shutter speed dial.

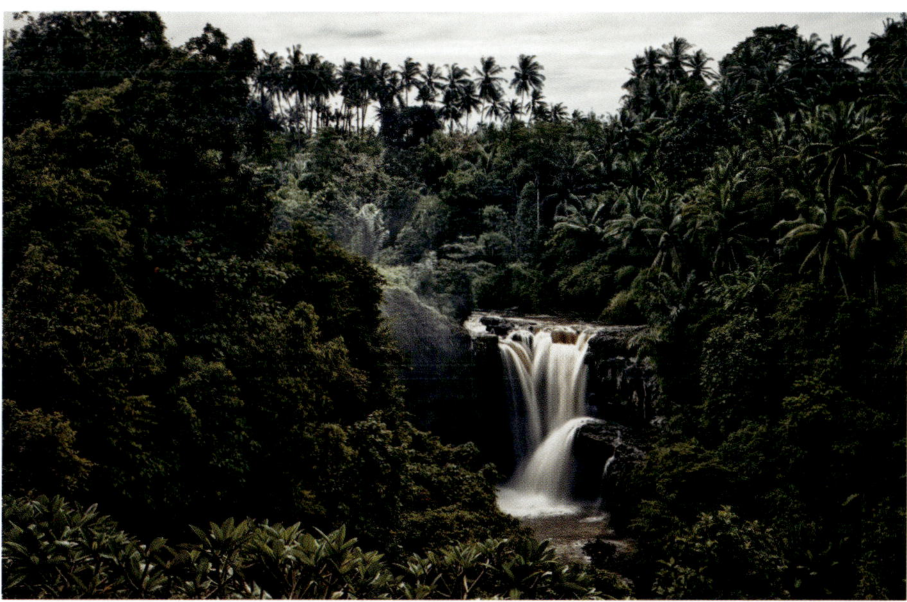

Fig. 37:  This **HDR image** consists of seven JPEGs (each taken with an exposure difference of 1 EV) that were merged in HDR Efex Pro by NIK/Google

<table><tr><td>**TIP 62**</td><td>**Using the electronic shutter**</td></tr></table>

The electronic shutter (ES) of the X-T10 offers three major advantages: it is completely silent, it eliminates vibrations from shutter shock, and it allows shutter speeds as fast as 1/32000s. That's great in situations where you want to be particularly stealthy, or when you want to use fast lenses like the XF56mmF1.2 R with wide-open aperture in bright light and spare yourself the hassle of attaching a ND filter.

You can set which shutter type the camera is supposed to use in SHOOTING MENU > SHUTTER TYPE, where three options are available:

- **MS:** The camera is only using the mechanical shutter. This is the default setting and also my recommended standard setting.

- **ES:** This setting switches the X-T10 to its electronic shutter with available shutter speeds between 1s and 1/32000s, and ISO settings between 200 and 6400. You cannot fire a flash when the ES is in use, and in burst mode the camera will only focus on the first frame of a series. This means that AF-C isn't able to track moving subjects in burst mode.

- **MS+ES:** In this mode, the camera combines both shutter types. It will automatically use the ES for shutter speeds faster than 1/4000s. Flash photography is only possible within the envelope of the mechanical shutter. In burst mode, the camera will only focus on the first frame of a series. This means that AF-C isn't able to track moving subjects in burst mode.

To set shutter speeds faster than 1/4000s, select 1/4000s with the shutter speed dial, then turn the front command dial to the right. Alternatively, you can set the shutter speed dial to **T** and access all available shutter speeds with the front command dial in 1/3 EV steps.

Please note that even at 1/32000s, the electronic shutter needs about 1/10s to capture all image contents. In other words, it takes the electronic shutter 1/10s to record all 16.3 megapixels of the sensor. This effect, known as Rolling Shutter, can lead to weird distortions when you are taking pictures of fast-moving subjects. In addition to that, image quality can deteriorate when the ES is used in concert with pulsing or flickering artificial light sources. The long read-out time and the rolling shutter are also responsible for the restrictions regarding flash photography and the camera's inability to track moving subjects with AF-C in burst mode.

With the electronic shutter, the X-T10 also can't perform a dark-frame subtraction for slow shutter speeds. That's why the slowest available electronic shutter speed is 1s. It may also be worth mentioning that regardless of your shutter type setting, the camera will always use the mechanical shutter to shoot Motion Panoramas.

Since the electronic shutter is completely silent, the camera is generating an artificial shutter sound when the ES is in use. The nature and volume of this sound effect can be set in SET-UP > SOUND SET-UP, where you can also entirely switch-off any artificial shutter sounds.

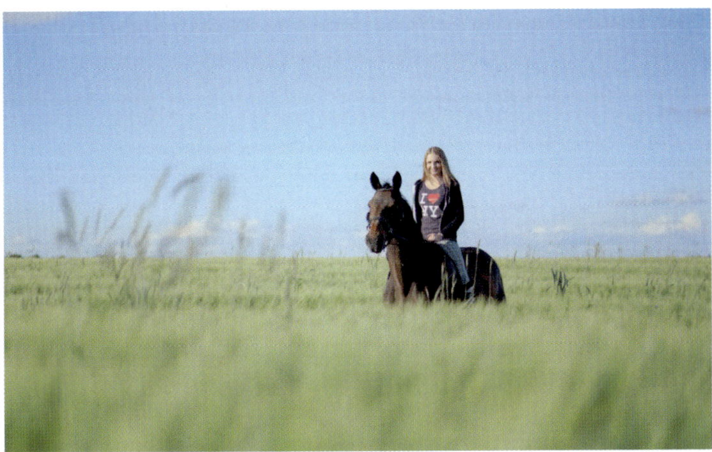

Fig. 38: The **electronic shutter** is a practical option for shots taken with fast lenses in bright light, when 1/4000s simply isn't fast enough to avoid overexposure

## 2.4 FOCUSING WITH THE X-T10

CDAF, PDAF, hybrid AF, zone AF? It can be quite confusing, since the X-T10 features a hybrid autofocus system that combines CDAF and PDAF:

- CDAF means **C**ontrast **D**etection **A**uto**F**ocus and is the current standard in mirrorless cameras. CDAF is available throughout the entire sensor area (49 AF frames in Single Point mode or 77 AF frames in Zone and Wide/Tracking mode) and works quite precisely, but is not particularly fast.

- PDAF means **P**hase **D**etection **A**uto**F**ocus and is the current standard in DSLRs. Since the X-T10 is mirrorless, its PDAF works directly on the sensor, but is only available throughout the nine (respectively 15) central AF frames. PDAF is pretty fast and particularly good at tracking moving subjects. It can predict where a moving object will be a split second from now, a feature that can be quite useful when you shoot in burst mode.

**Hybrid AF** means that the X-T10 combines both methods (CDAF and PDAF) by automatically picking the best method for the current subject and the current light conditions.

| | |
|---|---|
| **TIP 63** | **CDAF and PDAF:** what's the difference? |

Both AF methods offer distinct qualities that can be useful during your daily shooting:

- CDAF focuses on surfaces and works best with areas that offer a lot of contrast. A solid white or black wall doesn't work well with CDAF, but a checkered wall works great. It's the same with clothes: unicolor may not work, but patterned clothes work wonderfully. CDAF operates with a trial-and-error approach: it keeps adjusting the focus until it finds the distance setting with the utmost contrast. CDAF doesn't directly go to the optimal focus setting, which results in heightened autofocus motor activity and visible focus hunting, because the AF is going back and forth until it finds the optimal focus position.

■ PDAF in the X-T10 loves focusing on edges, especially vertical edges (or horizontal ones if you hold the camera upright). Unlike CDAF, PDAF is able to directly determine the distance to an object, so there's no need for focus hunting. That's why PDAF is considerably faster.

■ Both methods depend on good light to work with maximum efficiency. The brighter a scene is and the more contrast it has, the better. This means that bright lenses with large maximum aperture openings are beneficial, because they allow the AF to work with more light and less depth of field. The latter also helps increase the precision of the CDAF. It's worth noting that most lenses are less bright near their edges than they are in their center (this effect is called vignetting), so in bad lighting, the CDAF may work less efficiently with AF frames that are located far off the center.

| AF-S or AF-C? | TIP 64 |
| --- | --- |

Your X-T10 features two basic AF modes that can be selected with the focus selector at the front of the camera:

■ **AF-S (AF Single) is meant for stationary subjects.** Once you half-press the shutter button, the camera will focus on the object covered by the active AF frame and lock the distance as long as you keep the shutter button half-depressed. Then, you can either fully press the shutter button to take the shot, or you can take your finger off the shutter release and try again.

- **AF-C (AF Continuous) is meant for moving subjects,** especially those that move toward or away from the camera. When you half-press the shutter button, the camera starts focusing on the object covered by the active AF frame and continuously adjusts the distance to the moving object as long as you keep the shutter button half-depressed. In the viewfinder, this may look like the camera is continuously hunting, while the green AF confirmation dot in the bottom-left corner of the screen keeps going on and off. Don't worry! This is normal: the hybrid AF (PDAF and CDAF) has a pretty good track record of getting the moving object in focus when the shutter button is finally fully depressed. Just make sure that the active AF frame or AF zone always covers the part of the image that is supposed to be in focus. Don't forget that PDAF (with its predictive tracking capability) is only available in concert with one of the central AF frames. Prediction is quite useful with objects that are moving fast toward or away from the camera. Every camera experiences a small delay between pressing the shutter and actually recording the image. This shutter lag can be taken into account by the predictive PDAF: the camera isn't focusing on the object's current position, but on the position the object is *predicted* to be when the image is actually captured. Please note that predictive autofocus is also possible with CDAF, though to a lesser degree of performance.

- While AF-C is always focusing using the set working aperture, AF-S can open up the aperture beyond the working aperture to improve the AF performance in poor light. This also improves focusing accuracy due to the reduced depth of field caused by the wide-open aperture.

<table>
<tr><td>AF modes:<br>Single Point AF vs. Zone AF vs. Wide/Tracking AF</td><td>TIP 65</td></tr>
</table>

In SHOOTING MENU > AF MODE (or in the Quick menu) you can choose between SINGLE POINT, ZONE, or WIDE/TRACKING autofocus:

- **Single Point AF** mode is my recommended AF setting for most applications. In this mode, you have to manually select one of 49 available AF frames. Try to avoid old habits like using only the central frame in concert with the focus and recompose technique you have used with older cameras (typically DSLRs). It's better to compose the shot and *then* select a suitable AF frame that covers the part of the image that needs to be in perfect focus. This helps you avoid focus errors that invariably occur when you pan the focus plane to the left or right or up or down. Such focus errors may be irrelevant with long focal lengths and small aperture openings (large depth of field), but they can be quite unpleasant with wide-angle lenses, a wide aperture opening (small DOF), and short distances between the camera and the subject. Single Point AF can be used in concert with both AF-S and AF-C.

- You can think of **Zone AF** is an extension of Single Point AF. Basically, an AF zone is a particularly large AF frame that consists of a set of smaller AF points. Zones are available in sizes that cover 5×3, 3×3, or 5×5 out of a total of 77 AF points. Like Single Point AF frames, AF zones can be moved around within the image area. Since they are larger, AF zones make it easier to focus on moving subjects. In Zone AF mode, the camera will start looking for something to focus on in the center (crosshairs) of the selected zone and then expand its search toward the edges of the zone until it finds a target. Like Single Point AF, Zone AF works in concert with either AF-S or AF-C.

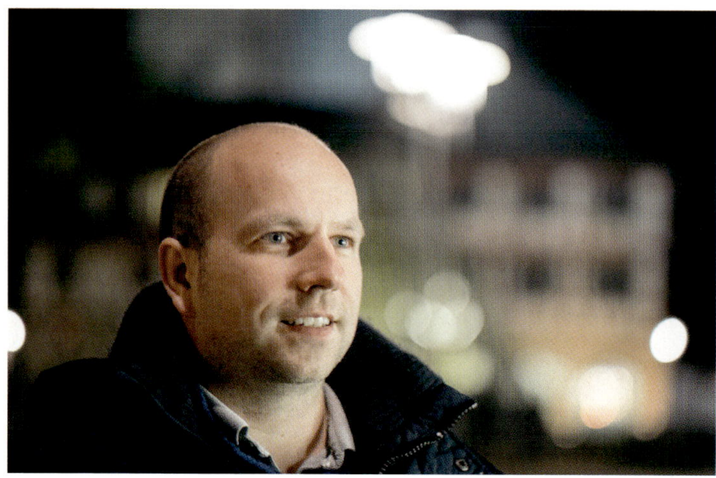

Fig. 39: Shooting with minimal depth of field, you can't really afford to use a focus and recompose habit because it would quickly lead to soft results that appear out of focus. Instead, compose the shot and *then* focus using a single autofocus frame (there are 49 to choose from in Single Point AF mode) that covers the part of the image that is supposed to be in focus.

■ When you combine **Wide/Tracking AF** mode with **AF-S,** the camera scans the entire image frame and automatically selects up to 9 of 77 available AF frames. It's a bit like rolling dice, since the camera is looking for areas with a lot of contrast. It doesn't know what's important in a scene. This changes when Wide/Tracking is used in concert with **AF-C:** this combination offers real 3D tracking of moving objects—that is, objects that not only move toward or away from the camera, but also left/right and up/down within the image frame. In order to track such an object, select Wide/Tracking and AF-C and pick one of the 77 available AF points. To start the tracking process, make sure that the selected point covers the moving object that you want to track, then half-press the shutter button to start the tracking process. As long as you keep the shutter-button half-pressed, the camera will automatically follow the selected subject with a cloud of AF frames as it moves across the image area.

Please note that Fujifilm has released a free *AF Handbook* detailing the new autofocus modes and mode combinations that come with your X-T10. You can download this useful brochure as a PDF at the following website: http://www.fujifilm.com/products/digital_cameras/pdf/x_t1_x_t10_af_handbook_01.pdf.

In addition to that, I have published a blog article describing the new AF features. You can read it here: http://www.fujirumors.com/using-firmware-4/. This article also contains links to short videos with examples of Single Point AF, Zone AF, and Wide/Tracking AF.

<table><tr><td>Selecting an AF frame or AF zone</td><td>TIP 66</td></tr></table>

The X-T10 offers an indirect and a direct method to select one of its 49 available AF frames in Single Point AF, or to move around an AF zone in Zone AF:

- The *indirect* method requires you to *first* press the AF button and *then* use the selector buttons to pick an AF frame or move an AF zone. Since the X-T10 doesn't feature a hard-wired AF button, you have to assign this function to one of the Fn buttons. By default, the lower selector button (arrow down button) serves as the AF button, but you can easily change that by pressing and holding another Fn button until its configuration menu pops up. Then you can select FOCUS AREA.

- The *direct* method doesn't require you to press the AF button before you can select an AF frame. Instead, the four selector buttons will immediately let you change the AF frame or move an AF zone. This may save you valuable time, but at the expense of losing four of the camera's Fn buttons. To set the X-T10 to direct AF frame selection, select SET-UP > BUTTON/DIAL SETTING > SELECTOR BUTTON SETTING > FOCUS AREA. You can reverse this setting anytime (and reactivate the four lost Fn buttons) by selecting SET-UP > BUTTON/DIAL SETTING > SELECTOR BUTTON SETTING > Fn BUTTON.

Not only does the X-T10 offer 49 different AF frames in Single Point AF, but each frame also comes in five different sizes. You can change the size of an AF frame by pressing the AF button (or any selector button if you are using the direct AF frame selection method) and then turning the command dial left or right to decrease or increase its size.

AF frame size affects the efficiency of both CDAF and PDAF. Here's a basic rule for you:

- Make your AF frame *as large as possible* and *as small as necessary*.

This is why:

- With a larger AF frame size, the camera has more to work with and a better chance to find contrast, especially when the light conditions aren't optimal.

- With a large AF frame size, there's also a higher chance for the camera to be able to use the faster PDAF method when one of the nine central AF frames is active. When PDAF isn't available, the camera will fall back to the slower CDAF.

- With a smaller AF frame size, the autofocus becomes more accurate. A small AF frame gives you better control over what *exactly* the camera is focusing on. Most of all, you should avoid AF frame sizes that are larger than the part of your image that needs to be in focus. For example, if your AF frame is larger than the head of the person you are focusing on, there's a chance that the camera will instead focus on the background behind their head, especially if that background contains a lot of contrast.

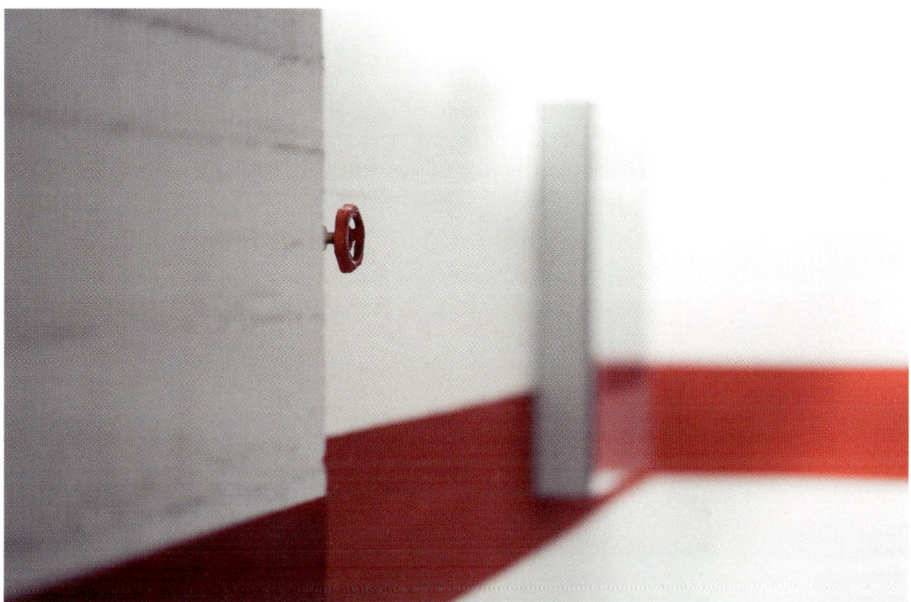

Fig. 40:  To get tiny parts of an image in perfect focus, it's best to choose a small AF frame size

In a similar fashion, you can change the size of AF zones by pressing the AF button (or any selector button if you are using the direct AF frame selection method) and then turning the command dial left or right to decrease or increase its size. You have a choice of three AF zone sizes: 5×3 (default), 3×3, or 5×5 out of 77 frames.

Since we can regard AF zones as very large AF frames, the same rules apply: larger zones are more convenient, and they potentially offer a faster AF response; but they are also potentially less accurate than smaller zones.

Keep in mind that the faster PDAF method is only available if the zone doesn't extend beyond the central 5×3 AF point matrix, so picking a large zone size of 5×5 will *always* force the camera to use the slower CDAF option. This is also true for smaller zones that partly extend into the CDAF-only area of the sensor.

In other words: as soon as an AF zone is configured to include at least one CDAF-only AF point, the focus system will switch to CDAF.

How do you know which AF points are PDAF-enabled and which points are CDAF-only? It's simple: in Single Point AF mode, the nine central AF frames are highlighted with a white cross to show that they are PDAF-enabled. In Zone AF mode, the 15 central AF points are displayed as larger squares than the surrounding 62 points.

<table><tr><td>TIP 68</td><td>Manual focus and DOF zone focusing</td></tr></table>

To set the camera to manual focus, move the focus selector at the front of your X-T10 to the M position. There are several manual focus aids available:

- A magnification tool with two different magnification levels

- Focus peaking (Focus Peak Highlight) with two different strength levels and optional colors (red or blue)

- Digital split image

- An electronic distance scale with depth-of-field bars

- One-Touch-AF (or Instant AF): autofocus in MF with the AF-L button

The digital distance scale can help you define a focus zone with predetermined depth of field (DOF). Everything within the DOF zone will look pixel-sharp even when the image is magnified to a 100% view. Please don't confuse manual zone focusing with Zone AF—they are completely different and not related to each other.

Here's a zone-focusing example: using an 18mm lens, manually set a distance of 15 feet and stop down to f/5.6. The DOF bars will show a depth-of-field zone that begins at around 12 feet and ends at around 30 feet. This means that everything located in this zone (between 12 and 30 feet) will appear equally in focus in the final image. All you have to do is make sure that your subject is within that zone when you press the shutter button.

A special case of zone focusing is setting the hyperfocal distance. This is the distance setting with the maximum DOF, including infinity. Again, the electronic DOF scale can be very helpful: all you have to do is manually set the distance where the blue DOF bar on the right touches the infinity mark. For example, using an 18mm lens at f/16, the hyperfocal distance is at about 15 feet, with the pixel-sharp DOF zone extending from seven feet to infinity.

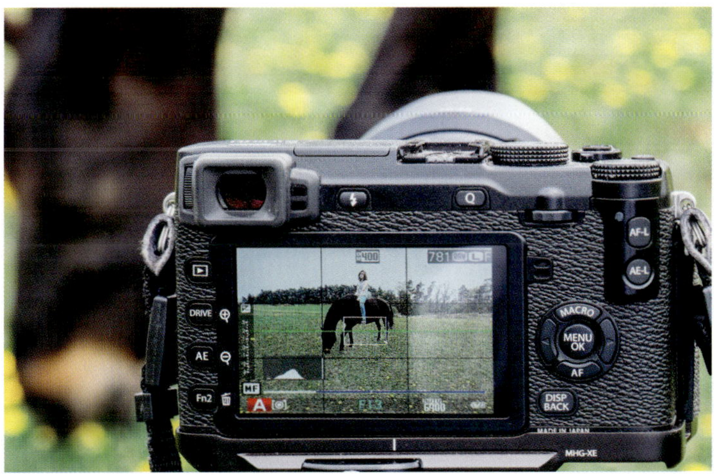

Fig. 41: Setting the hyperfocal distance with the electronic distance and DOF scale: instead of focusing on a predetermined distance, manually change the focus distance until the blue DOF bar touches the infinity mark on the right end of the scale. This gives us the hyperfocal distance for a given aperture and focal length. This image shows an X-E2 (the scale is similar to the one on the X-T10).

Please note that depth of field is very much dependent on the circle of confusion (CoC) that is used for its calculation. Fujifilm uses a very conservative CoC that guarantees pixel-sharp results even when the DOF zone is viewed at 100% magnification on a computer screen. Fuji is literally using the sensor's maximum resolution as a benchmark. Everything that's located within the electronic DOF zone will be rendered at least as sharp as the sensor can resolve it. In the age of pixel peeping, this is as good as it can get.

It's important to know that the engraved analog distance and DOF scales on the XF14mmF2.8, XF16mmF1.4, and XF23mmF1.4 lenses follow a different rule. They are based on a less conservative circle of confusion that is about two aperture stops more generous than the electronic scale. In order to determine the pixel-sharp DOF at f/8 with one of these lenses, you should look at the engraved markers for f/4.

<table><tr><td>TIP 69</td><td>Manual focus assistants: focus peaking and digital split image</td></tr></table>

The X-T10 features two MF assistants:

- **Focus peaking** (or Focus Peak Highlight) emphasizes the edges of objects when they are in focus. This method is especially useful in concert with longer focal lengths and bright lenses with a tiny DOF.

- **Digital split image** tries to simulate the split image indicator of analog SLRs. It works best with vertical lines (or horizontal lines when the camera is held in portrait orientation). It uses the sensor's PDAF-enabled area, which is why the digital split image is just as large as the area covered by the central AF frames.

To quickly switch between the two MF assistants, you can press and hold the rear command dial for about a second while you are in MF mode.

You can watch a short video demonstrating the manual focus assistants here: www.youtube.com/watch?v=7FR3l6S12JA.

<table><tr><td>Focus check: use the **magnifier tool!**</td><td>TIP 70</td></tr></table>

The magnifier tool is helpful for checking whether or not the current focus is spot-on. Simply press the rear command dial (either in AF-S / Single Point AF or in MF mode) to magnify everything that is covered by the active AF or MF frame.

In MF mode, you can even change the magnification level by turning the rear command dial. You can also combine the focus check with both MF assistants (focus peaking and digital split image). Please note that in digital split image mode, there's only *one* magnification level available.

By selecting SET-UP > SCREEN SET-UP > FOCUS CHECK > ON, the magnifier tool is *automatically* activated when you turn the manual focus ring of a lens in MF mode. You can immediately cancel any automatic focus check by half-pressing the shutter button.

Similar to the AF-S and AF-C modes, there are 49 different MF frames in manual focus mode. These frames indicate which part of the image will be magnified when focus check is activated. As usual, you can change the active frame by pressing the AF button and then moving the MF frame around with the selector keys.

<table><tr><td>**One-Touch-AF** (Instant AF)</td><td>TIP 71</td></tr></table>

One-Touch-AF (or Instant AF) allows you to use autofocus in manual focus mode. All you have to do is press the AF-L button. One-Touch-AF always works with a wide-open aperture and works with both PDAF and CDAF. Like normal autofocus, its efficiency also depends on the size of the selected focus frame.

One-Touch-AF is the most precise AF method available, which also makes it a bit slower than the camera's normal autofocus. It can be combined with conventional manual focusing: you can use One-Touch-AF to quickly autofocus on an object, then manually fine-tune the focus by turning the focus ring and using MF assistants like the magnifier and/ or focus peaking. Please note that this convenient method is *not* available when you are using lenses with manual focus clutches (XF14mmF2.8, XF16mmF1.4, or XF23mmF1.4).

One-Touch-AF normally works like AF-S, but you can also set it to continuous focus with SHOOTING MENU > AUTOFOCUS SETTING > INSTANT AF SETTING > AF-C. In this setting, One-Touch-AF will track an object (using the set working aperture) as long as you keep the AF-L button depressed in manual focus mode.

| TIP 72 | Using **AF+MF** |

AF+MF enables you to focus in AF mode, then adjust the focus manually by turning the focus ring, all while holding the shutter button half-depressed. Select SHOOTING MENU > AUTOFOCUS SETTING > AF+MF > ON to enable this feature. In order to use AF+MF, your X-T10 has to be in AF-S autofocus mode.

Here's how it works:

- Autofocus on your subject as usual in AF-S mode by half-pressing the shutter button.

- Once the autofocus has been confirmed (green square[s]) or not confirmed (red AF warning), keep the shutter button half-depressed and rotate the focus ring of your lens to *manually* adjust the focus distance until you are satisfied.

- When you are happy with your manual focus adjustments, fully depress the half-pressed shutter button to take the shot.

I see three main applications for AF+MF:

- **Manual focus in situations when autofocus fails**: Instead of losing time by changing the focus mode from AF to MF, you can immediately focus manually when the camera's AF fails to acquire the subject. Simply adjust the focus manually using the focus ring. If Focus Peaking is enabled, it will automatically engage as soon as the focus ring is rotated and manual focus (MF) kicks in. You can also use the Focus Check function (SET-UP > SCREEN SET-UP > FOCUS CHECK > ON) to automatically magnify the focus area as soon as you turn the focus ring. To make this work, make sure that AF-S and SINGLE POINT AF are set. You can also combine Focus Check magnification with Focus Peaking.

- **Correcting the camera's autofocus**: There are instances when you might want to fine-tune the autofocus of your camera by adjusting it manually. Again, Focus Peaking is available to make things easier, and you can enable Focus Check to automatically show a magnified view of the focus area when you turn the focus ring. The magnification (either 2.5× or 6×) will be the same magnification level that is set in the camera's MF mode.

- **Shifting the depth-of-field (DOF) zone or setting the hyperfocal distance**: AF+MF let's you quickly shift the DOF zone toward or away from the camera by turning the focus ring after half-pressing the shutter button. The digital distance scale on the screen can be quite helpful here. For example, you can shift the right tip of the blue DOF bar to just touch the infinity mark of the digital distance scale to set the hyperfocal distance.

*Hint: After you have made manual focus adjustments using the automatic Focus Check magnification, you can get rid of the magnification and return to a full view of the scene by switching the camera to manual focus (MF) while still keep-*

*ing the shutter button half-depressed. Then fully depress the shutter button when the moment is right. A future firmware update could take care of this issue by allowing you to manually switch the magnifier on or off in AF+MF mode.*

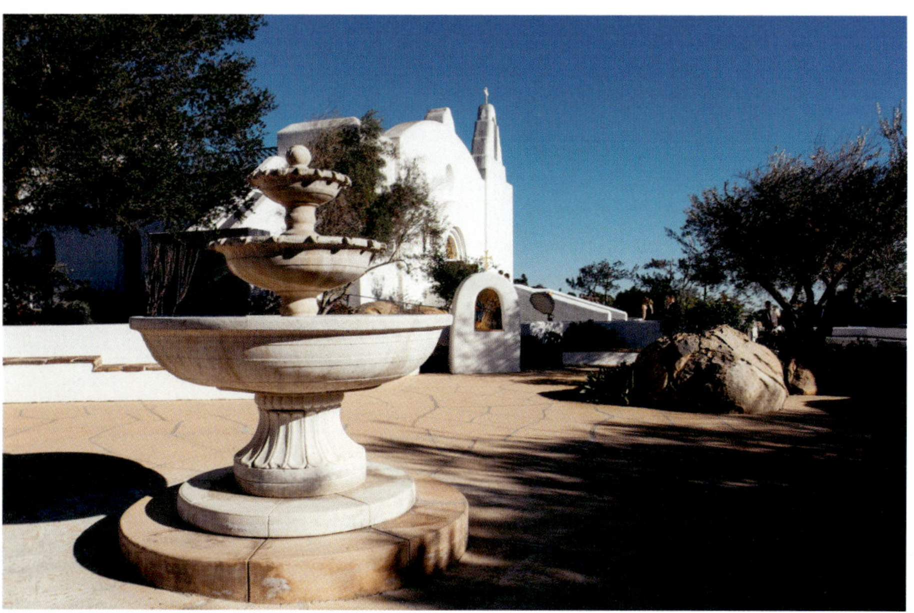

**Fig. 42:** In the example above, I autofocused on the fountain by placing the AF frame right over it. I used a small aperture of f/16 for plenty of depth of field (DOF). Since the portion of the DOF zone that extends in front of the fountain toward the camera is useless in this case, I manually shifted the DOF zone away from the camera using AF+MF. The resulting DOF zone starts at the fountain and extends all the way back.

At first glance, the MF component of AF+MF may look like your usual manual focus, but it's not. While genuine MF is always performed at wide-open aperture, the MF part of AF+MF is performed at the selected working aperture. That's because the shutter button is half-pressed, so the camera has already been primed to take the shot with minimal shutter lag.

This also means that the EVF/LCD will display a live view image that shows the actual depth of field of the resulting image. It means that Focus Peaking will show an increasingly larger zone as being in focus when you stop down the lens. This can make it more difficult to nail your manual focus adjustment.

AF+MF also works with clutch-type lenses such as the XF14mm, XF16mm, or XF23mm. These lenses feature a clutch to mechanically switch between MF and AF mode. Since the focus ring of these lenses can only be turned when the clutch is in the MF position, you need the following configuration to get AF+MF to work:

- Enable AF+MF in the shooting menu.

- Select AF-S in the camera (using the focus mode switch) and MF on the lens (by pulling the clutch mechanism toward the camera).

- Use AF+MF as described above.

Here are a few tips regarding AF+MF and clutch lenses:

- Make sure that the manual focus ring of the lens has sufficient play to the left and right so you can make the necessary MF adjustments.

- The distance and DOF markings on your clutch lens have no meaning in the AF+MF configuration. Instead, use the digital distance/DOF scale that's displayed in the camera's viewfinder or on the LCD.

- In order to use clutch lenses in genuine manual focus mode when AF+MF is on, both the lens *and* the camera have to be set to MF.

<table>
<tr><td>TIP 73</td><td>Pre-AF: a relic of the past</td></tr>
</table>

Pre-AF brings the AF-C of older Fujifilm X cameras (like the X-E1) to the X-T10: with Pre-AF set to on, the camera will always focus on whatever is covered by the active AF frame, even when the shutter button is *not* half-depressed.

Pre-AF burns plenty of power because the autofocus in the lens is always working. On the other hand, using it can potentially result in a quicker AF response. If you shoot a lot of action, Pre-AF may be helpful, but don't forget to pack a few extra batteries. Normally, I set this option (SHOOTING MENU > AUTOFOCUS SETTING > PRE-AF) to OFF.

That said, don't forget to *always* switch on High Performance mode (SET-UP > POWER MANAGEMENT > HIGH PERFORMANCE > ON).

<table>
<tr><td>TIP 74</td><td>Using face detection and eye-detection</td></tr>
</table>

Face detection is a combined autofocus and exposure metering mode. It even affects auto white balance. You can activate it with SHOOTING MENU > AUTOFOCUS SETTING > FACE DETECTION > ON.

Here's what it does:

- The camera scans the scene in the viewfinder and detects one or several human faces. It automatically focuses on one of the faces when the shutter button is half-pressed. When more than one face is detected, the camera tends to focus on the face that's closest to the center. That face will be highlighted with a green frame. The other detected faces will be highlighted with a white frame.

- Face detection uses a custom version of weighted multi metering that puts an emphasis on the selected face. The goal is to deliver an exposure with correct skin tones. It may also influence the camera's auto white balance.

Face detection is both a blessing and a curse. It's a blessing when it works because it focuses directly on a face and makes sure that it's correctly exposed. It's a curse when the detection goes wrong, because it doesn't just mean that the focus might miss; it may also mess up your exposure metering.

The good news: in most cases, face detection works, even with people who only show their profiles to the camera. The bad news: face detection may not work well on folks wearing glasses.

- I don't recommend using face detection in burst mode (it only works in the slower CL mode, anyway), because the exposure metering may change during the series of shots depending on whether or not a face is detected.

- If you want to take face detection exposure metering out of the equation, you can set the camera to manual exposure mode **M**. While metering will still be affected in this mode, the exposure itself will not.

- Face detection works with the full sensor area and thus only employs CDAF. PDAF and its predictive capabilities aren't available. This means that AF-C tracking of moving objects doesn't work as well as it could. In other words, face detection isn't the best option to track an athlete or a child running toward the camera. It's better to use the camera's conventional AF-C mode with one of the nine central AF frames or an appropriate AF zone.

- Spot and average metering aren't available when face detection is active. The camera is always using a derivate of multi metering.

- When face detection fails to detect a face in the scene, the camera will automatically fall back to the selected AF mode: Single Point, Zone, or Wide/Tracking. At the same time, exposure metering reverts back to regular multi metering.

- Neither AF-Lock nor AE-Lock is available when face detection is active.

- Face detection is not available in manual focus mode. However, you can still use it with adapted lenses as long as you set the camera to an AF mode and activate face detection. In this case, face detection will only work as an exposure metering mode.

- Face detection can be assigned to one of the X-T10's function (Fn) buttons. Personally, I tend to assign it to the Fn button at the back of the camera.

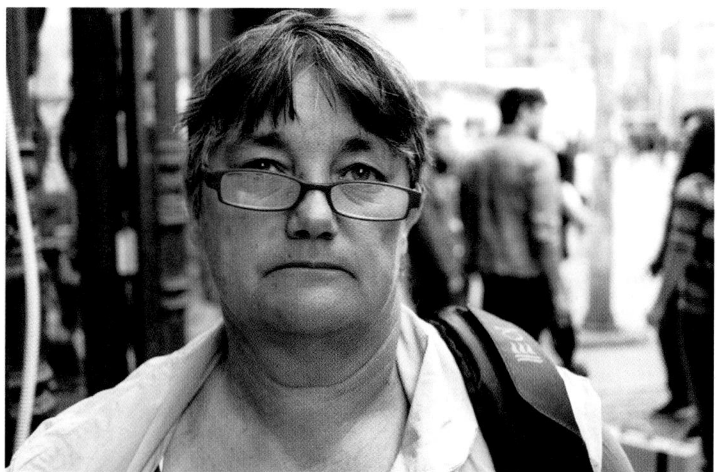

Fig. 43: **Face detection** is best for stationary scenes with one or more people looking at the camera. For people who are moving toward the camera, use one of the nine central AF frames or an AF zone in concert with the X-T10's tracking autofocus (AF-C).

The X-T10 improves face detection accuracy by adding an optional eye detection feature. Eye detection is only available in AF-S mode. To activate it, switch on face detection and then select SHOOTING MENU > AUTOFOCUS SETTING > EYE DETECTION AF, where you can tell the camera to focus on either the left or the right eye of your subject by selecting LEFT EYE PRIORITY or RIGHT EYE PRIORITY. Select AUTO to make the camera focus on the eye that's closest to the camera, or select OFF to deactivate eye detection.

In the viewfinder, the camera will highlight a detected eye within a detected face with a small square and focus on it when you half-press the shutter button. In my experience, it doesn't hurt to leave this feature on all the time. I usually set it to AUTO. However, don't forget that it's only available in AF-S mode and when face detection is switched on.

| Using **AF-Lock** | TIP 75 |
| --- | --- |

In AF-S mode, pressing the AF-Lock button focuses the camera and locks the distance. In SHOOTING MENU > AE/AF LOCK MODE, you can configure the button to function as an on/off switch or to work only as long as it is being pressed.

When AF-Lock is active, the camera won't refocus when the shutter button is half or fully depressed. Instead, it will keep the focus at the previously locked distance. This may be convenient when you want to take multiple shots of a non-moving subject in quick succession. With AF-Lock, you don't have to refocus every time to take another image. AF-Lock decouples autofocus and exposure metering: as long as AF-Lock is on, half-pressing the shutter button will only meter and lock the exposure, not the focus.

In a similar fashion, you can use the AE-Lock button to meter and lock exposure; in this case, half-pressing the shutter button will only change the focusing. You can even combine both AE-L and AF-L. In this case, half-pressing the shutter will only set the working aperture and prime the camera. There won't be any new metering for focus or exposure.

<table>
<tr><td>TIP 76</td><td>Focusing in poor light</td></tr>
</table>

Low light can quickly lead to poor contrast, making it difficult for the camera to find and lock the correct autofocus distance. However, the amount of light that reaches the sensor depends not only on the brightness of a scene, but also on the brightness of the lens. The XF56mmF1.2 is 3.5 stops or EVs (exposure values) brighter than the XF18–55mmF2.8–4 kit zoom in its 55mm position. In other words, with the XF56mmF1.2 lens, the world looks 3.5 stops brighter to the camera's autofocus system. You can guess which lens will perform better when the light gets difficult.

Don't be confused by appearances—it's true that the live view image in the viewfinder will look equally bright with both lenses, but that's only because the camera is electronically amplifying the live view display. Don't forget that autofocus needs real light and contrast. When the light is bad, it's vital to target surfaces with contrast and, if possible, use a larger AF frame size.

One way of tackling a bad lighting situation is by using fast lenses like the XF56mmF1.2, XF35mmF1.4, or XF23mmF1.4. You can also generate light—the camera's AF assist lamp can illuminate a subject to help the autofocus find better contrast. Be aware that the AF assist lamp can be easily blocked by your finger (depending on how you hold your camera) or by an attached lens hood. Watch for it, and remove the lens hood if necessary. Since the AF assist lamp tends to concentrate on the center of the image, it works best in concert with one of the more central AF frames. In order to use the AF assist lamp, make sure to set SHOOTING MENU > AUTOFOCUS SETTING > AF ILLUMINATOR > ON.

An alternative to using the AF assist lamp is using a flash light to temporarily illuminate a subject. If you are indoors, you can try turning on the lights in the room for a moment to use AF-Lock to lock the focus. Just make sure to meter the exposure *after* the lights are off again.

*Important: If you intend to stop down the aperture of your lens in poor lighting, make sure to use either AF-S or manual focus (Instant-AF) as your focus mode. Do not use AF-C, because this mode will focus with your stopped-down working aperture, which will make things difficult for your camera, since less light will reach the sensor.*

| **Macro:** focusing at close distances | TIP 77 |
| --- | --- |

The biggest challenge with shooting macro is the lack of DOF, or depth of field. The slightest movement may cause the shot to be out of focus. That's why macro photography is usually performed using a tripod and manual focus, often with One-Touch-AF, focus check (magnifier tool), and focus peaking. It's vital not to recompose after the focus has been set. To get a visual impression of the current DOF, you can half-press the shutter or assign PREVIEW DEPTH OF FIELD to one of the Fn buttons.

Macro shots usually require you to stop down the lens in order to increase the DOF. Since this can result in slower shutter speeds, it's important to make sure that the subject isn't moving too fast or out of the focus plane. Shooting a closeup of a flower in the wind may not yield excellent results.

If you don't want to use manual focus in macro mode, you can also focus automatically. Here's how:

- Set the focus selector switch to AF-S.

- Set Single Point AF and select the smallest AF frame size available.

- Reposition the small AF frame to exactly cover the part of the image that you want to be in focus. Quickly take the shot after you half-press the shutter—don't recompose.

- You can check your focus before taking a shot by pressing the rear command dial.

- Try not to shoot handheld; it is better to use a tripod.

- ■ Stop down the lens and visually check the depth of field by half-pressing the shutter button or using the DOF preview function that can be assigned to any Fn button.

- ■ Make sure there is sufficient light, and try to shoot subjects that don't move in and out of the focus plane.

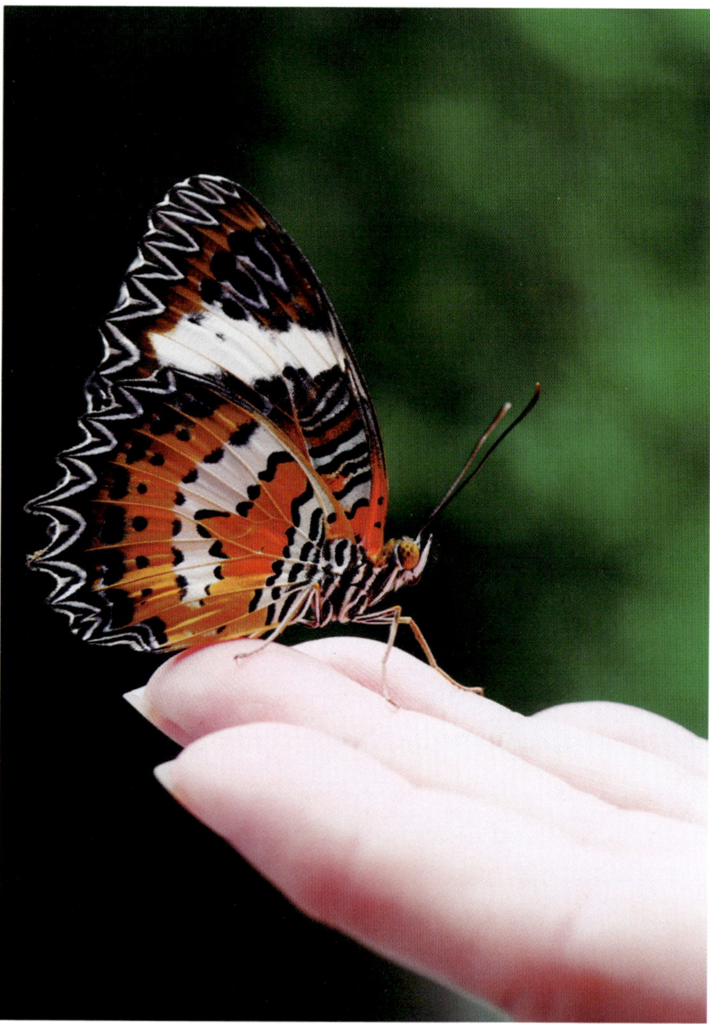

Fig. 44: **Macro shots** can be quite challenging due to their lack of DOF. That's why a tripod is highly recommended. With a little bit of luck, handheld shots are possible as well, like this snapshot, which was taken with an XF60mmF2.4 R.

You can add macro capability to many of your existing XF and XC lenses by using Fujifilm's electronic macro extension tubes: MCEX-11 or MCEX-16. The following website (www.fujifilm.com/products/digital_cameras/accessories/pdf/mcex_01.pdf) will provide a chart that shows you how these extension tubes enhance the magnification factor of each lens. Please note that the camera's electronic DOF/distance scale doesn't reflect the use of macro extension tubes.

<table><tr><td>Focusing on moving subjects (1): the "autofocus trick"</td><td>TIP 78</td></tr></table>

Rule of thumb: Use AF-S (Single) for stationary subjects that don't move toward or away from the camera; use AF-C (Continuous) for subjects that do move toward or away from the camera. But, as usual, there's no rule without an exception.

Meet the so-called "autofocus trick" or "shutter mash" technique:

- Set the focus selector switch to AF-S and the camera to single shot (set the DRIVE dial to S). Make sure that high-performance mode is on (SET-UP > POWER MANAGEMENT > HIGH PERFORMANCE > ON). Also make sure to use the mechanical shutter.

- Use Single Point AF or Zone AF and select an AF frame or AF zone position and size that cover the part of the moving subject that you want to be in focus. If possible, use the inner AF frames. As you know, these AF frames are PDAF-enabled. However, it's definitely possible to also use the outer frames that only operate with CDAF. If your composition requires them, go for it!

- Set a suitable exposure and make sure that the shutter speed is fast enough to avoid unwanted motion blur. Most action shots require shutter speeds of at least 1/500s.

- Follow the moving subject in the viewfinder, making sure that the selected AF frame or AF zone always covers the part that needs to be in focus. Do *not* half-press the shutter button!

- *Fully* depress the shutter button in one swift motion when you want to take the shot. The camera will need some time to focus, so make sure that the AF frame stays positioned over the moving subject while the camera is focusing. As soon as the camera is able to lock the focus, it will automatically take the shot. This (the time between fully depressing the shutter and the camera taking the shot) can take a good fraction of a second.

The AF trick or shutter mash is based on the camera's autofocus priority logic. When you release the shutter, the camera *first* attempts to lock the focus, *then* take the shot. Since the delay between having locked the focus and re-leasing the shutter is very short, the moving subject ends up being in focus most of the time. This means that the AF trick works best with aperture settings that offer sufficient depth of field, and with subjects that don't move too fast toward the camera.

A negative aspect of this method is the fact that there's a delay between fully depressing the shutter button and the camera taking the shot. This delay occurs because the camera needs time to establish focus on the subject. This makes it challenging to hit decisive moments, and requires some amount of foresight from the photographer.

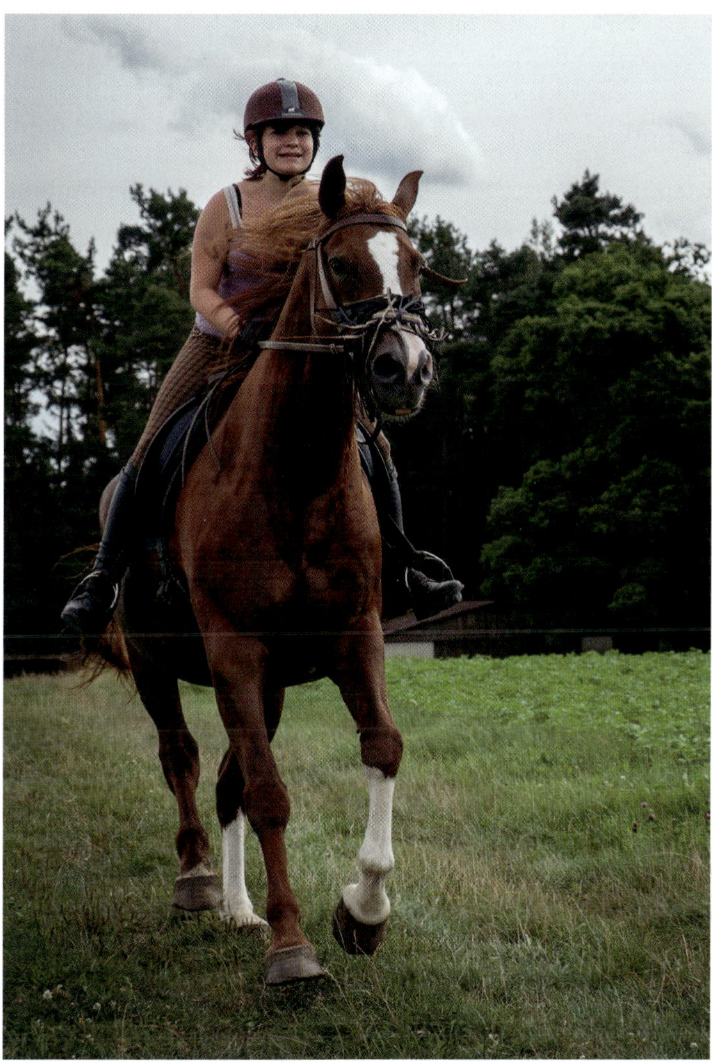

Fig. 45: A running horse captured using the **autofocus trick** or shutter mash technique. With older X-mount models like the X-Pro1, X-E1, X-M1, or X-A1, this method is the only way to capture subjects (using the camera's autofocus) that are moving toward the camera. This sample image was taken with an X-E1.

<table><tr><td>**TIP 79**</td><td>Focusing on moving subjects (2): **the focus trap**</td></tr></table>

Setting up a focus trap is about prefocusing on a location that a moving object will eventually pass through. This method can be useful with sports and other action that runs along a predetermined course (track, street, trail, etc.).

This is how it works:

- Set the camera to manual focus (MF) using the focus selector switch. Make sure to use the mechanical shutter.

- Prefocus on the location where you want to capture the moving subject. Select an aperture with sufficient depth of field (DOF) to make sure that all relevant parts of the object will be in focus.

- Half-press the shutter button when the moving object is approaching the location that you have in focus. The camera will lock the exposure and set the working aperture.

- Fully depress the shutter as soon as the object is about to cross the location that you have in focus.

There's only a very small shutter lag between half-pressing and fully depressing the shutter button. Depending on how fast the object is moving, it may be necessary to fully depress the shutter button a split second early.

Alternatively, you can set the camera to burst mode (set the DRIVE dial to CH). With this setting, the X-T10 takes about eight frames per second (fps), so there's a good chance that one or two of them will capture your fast-moving subject as it crosses your focus trap.

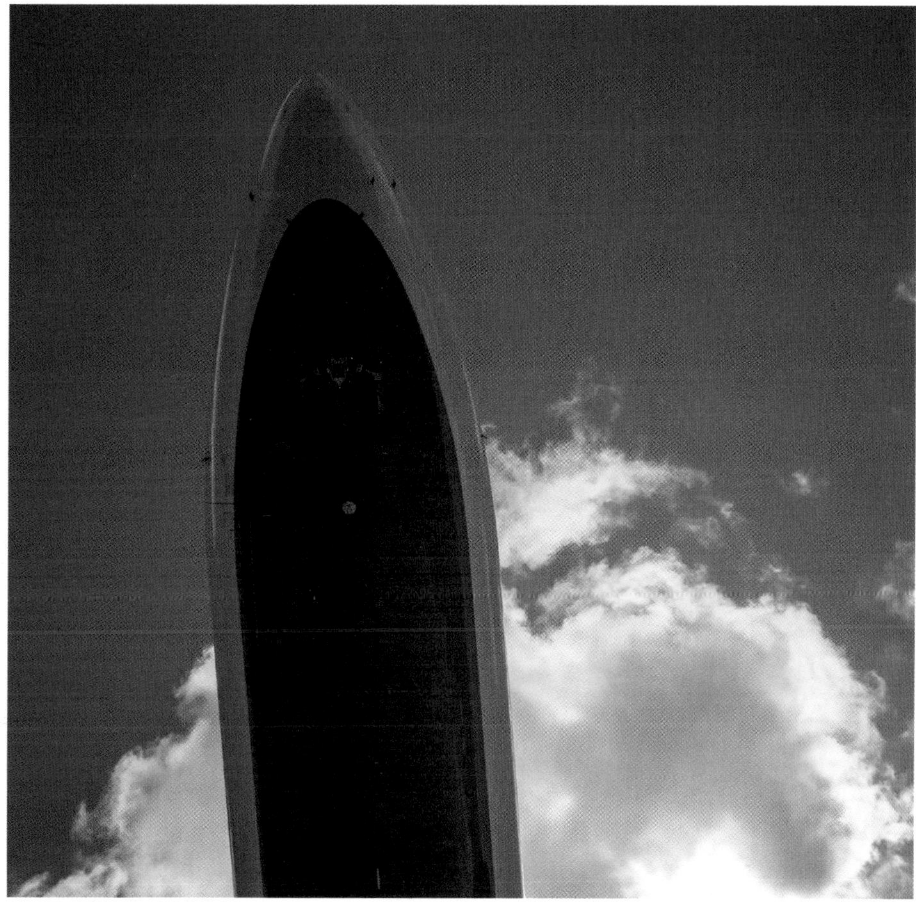

Fig. 46: **Focus trap:** To capture this landing Airbus A330 as it was flying over me at a distance of only a few meters, timing was essential. Instead of using autofocus, I prefocused my 18mm lens with sufficient depth of field and waited for the right moment with my camera primed and the shutter half-pressed.

You can also trap your moving subjects in a set-up focus zone. Stop down your lens enough to create a sufficiently large DOF zone, and then wait until a subject enters the zone. This method is often used by street photographers with wide-angle lenses (typically 18–23mm) who can't afford to miss the decisive moment.

A variant of this method is panning the camera with a slow shutter speed and a small aperture (plenty of DOF). The slow shutter speed makes sure that the background is blurred, while the subject remains in focus.

When panning with a lens that features optical image stabilization (OIS), you should switch off the OIS.

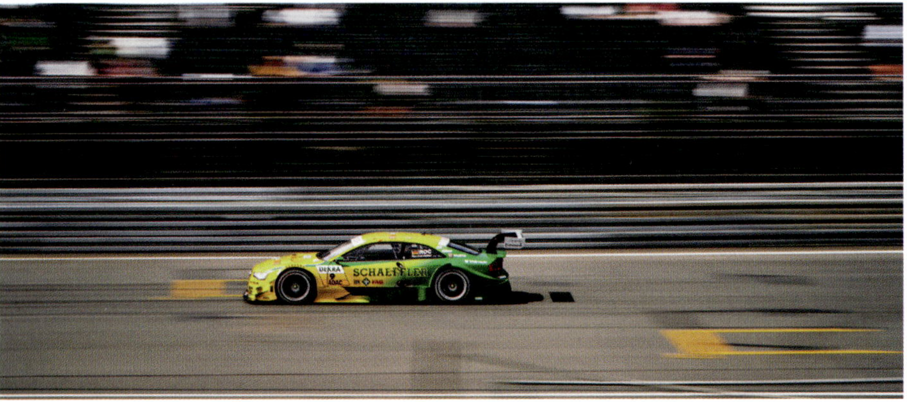

Fig. 47: **Panning** the camera in-sync with a racecar at 1/60s: the slow shutter speed resulted in f/20 and more than sufficient DOF using the XF60mmF2.4 R lens

**TIP 80**   Focusing on moving subjects (3): **Autofocus tracking using Single Point AF, Zone AF, or Wide/Tracking AF**

The predictive PDAF of your X-T10 uses the nine (in Single Point AF) or 15 (in Zone AF) central AF points. Predictive PDAF allows you to track moving subjects with your camera in three-dimensional space. Since the camera is able to calculate the movement of the object, it can automatically prefocus on its future position and compensate for any inherent shutter lag.

The X-T10 also improves the predictive capabilities of the CDAF. This means that subject tracking is also available with AF frames that surround the central PDAF points, as long as the burst rate in continuous shooting mode doesn't exceed three frames per second.

It's important to note that the hit rate of such predictions is never near 100%. However, it's usually high enough to deliver good results in concert with the camera's burst mode settings.

Let's start with the **Single Point AF** and **Zone AF** modes:

■ Set the focus mode selector switch to AF-C and make sure that high performance mode is on (SET-UP > POWER MANAGEMENT > HIGH PERFORMANCE > ON). Also make sure that the shutter type is set to the mechanical shutter (MS) in the shooting menu.

■ Set the camera to burst mode (DRIVE dial to CL or CH). I recommend using the slower CL mode, as it displays a real-time live view image between shots and supports all AF frames.

■ If you are using Single Point AF, select one of the nine central autofocus frames (SHOOTING MENU > AUTO-FOCUS SETTING > FOCUS AREA). If you use one of the 40 outer AF frames, the camera will only use CDAF. In concert with one of the 40 outer AF frames, you can only use the slower of the two burst modes (CL). You should still get pretty good results, though.

■ If you are using Zone AF, select a zone that doesn't extend beyond the central 5×3 AF point matrix (SHOOTING MENU > AUTOFOCUS SETTING > FOCUS AREA). If you use a zone that includes AF points beyond this PDAF-enabled area, the camera can only use CDAF, and only the slower of the two burst modes (CL) is available.

■ Position the selected AF frame or AF zone to directly cover the subject or part of the subject that you want to be in focus. If you are using Zone AF, make sure that the central crosshair of the selected zone covers the part of the subject you want to focus on. Now half-press the shutter button, and the camera will start tracking the subject that is covered by the AF frame or AF zone.

- Keep the shutter button half-depressed as you follow the moving subject with the selected AF frame or AF zone.

- Fully depress the shutter when you want to start taking a series of exposures. The actual burst speed (frame rate) depends on how well the camera is able to track the subject. As the camera is taking pictures, always try to keep the selected AF frame or AF Zone covering the part of your image that is supposed to be in focus. This may be challenging at first, so practicing is important.

In the above configuration with burst mode and AF-C, the X-T10 is still adjusting the exposure between shots. However, white balance and dynamic range settings are determined with the first shot and remain constant throughout the series.

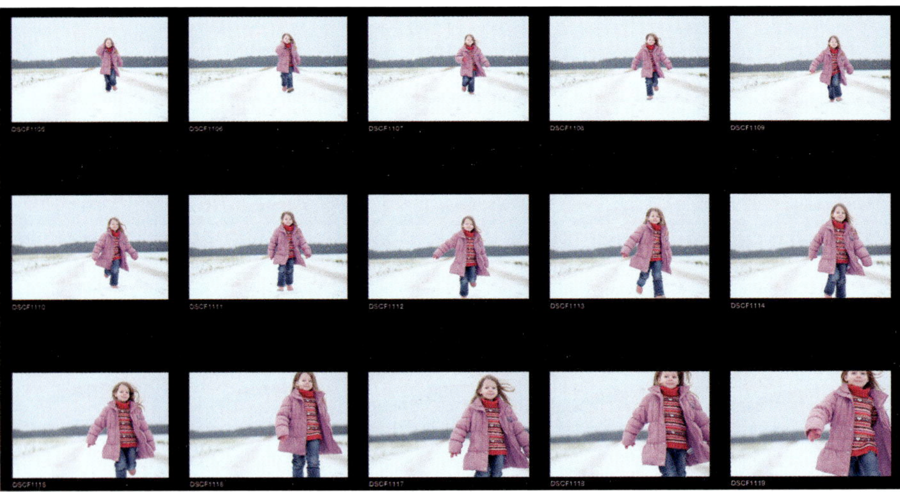

Fig. 48: **AF tracking** at eight frames per second: The predictive autofocus was tracking the girl with the selected AF frame while she was running toward the camera. To make this work, it's vital to follow the subject with the active AF frame or AF zone, making sure the AF frame or zone is always covering the part of the subject that is supposed to be in focus.

In principle, AF tracking also works in single shot mode. In this case, the camera takes a single frame when the shutter button is fully depressed, then ends the tracking.

By the way, it is perfectly normal for the hybrid AF to continuously hunt in the viewfinder during focus tracking (in AF-C mode). Don't be irritated by the live view image changing between in focus and not in focus. It's all about the result being in focus.

As an alternative to Single Point and Zone AF, you can also use **Wide/Tracking AF** in concert with AF-C to track a moving subject. This mode enables real 3D tracking, meaning the camera isn't merely tracking a subject's changing distance to the camera (z-axis), but also its left/right (x-axis) and up/down (y-axis) movement within the image frame.

Here's how it works:

■ Set the focus mode selector switch to AF-C and make sure that high performance mode is on (SET-UP > POWER MANAGEMENT > HIGH PERFORMANCE > ON). Also make sure that the shutter type is set to the mechanical shutter (MS) in the shooting menu.

■ Set the camera to **Wide/Tracking AF** and select the slower of the two burst modes (DRIVE dial to CL). That way, 3D tracking will be available for the *entire* image frame, but it will only track objects using CDAF. If you set the DRIVE dial to CH, tracking will use PDAF, but will be limited to the much smaller PDAF-enabled central area. In my experience, CDAF tracking works quite well—that's why I recommend using the slower but wider (and hence more flexible) CDAF option.

■ Select one of the 77 available tracking AF points (SHOOTING MENU > AUTOFOCUS SETTING > FOCUS AREA). The point you select will serve as a starting point for your tracking action, so position it in a way that suits your composition.

- To identify your target, make sure that the selected AF point covers the object that you want to track and half-press the shutter button. As long as you keep the shutter button half-depressed, the camera will use pattern recognition to automatically follow the object as it moves around the frame (or as you move the camera around) with a cloud of green AF frames.

- Fully depress the shutter button and keep it pressed to take pictures at the selected burst rate.

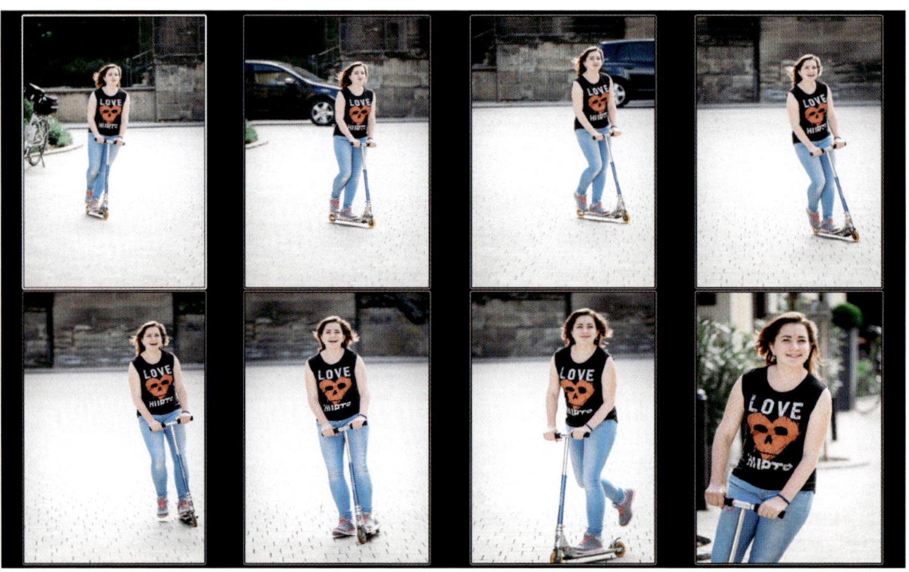

Fig. 49: AF-C in concert with WIDE/TRACKING and burst mode can track a subject in 3-dimensional space. To accomplish this, the X-T10 is using pattern recognition to follow the designated subject as it moves around.

| TIP 81 | Focus priority vs. Release priority |
| --- | --- |

The autofocus in your X-T10 will *always* try to focus on a subject first before the camera takes the shot. In this context, release priority vs. focus priority only refers to how the camera is behaving when the AF *fails* to lock on a target:

- Set SHOOTING MENU > AUTOFOCUS SETTING > RELEASE/FOCUS PRIORITY > AF-S PRIORITY SELECTION > FOCUS to stop the camera from taking a picture when the autofocus (AF-S) can't lock onto a target (red AF warning).

- Set SHOOTING MENU > AUTOFOCUS SETTING > RELEASE/ FOCUS PRIORITY > AF-C PRIORITY SELECTION > FOCUS to make sure that the X-T10 only takes pictures in AF-C mode (particularly in concert with burst mode), when the autofocus is able to lock onto something.

Basically, selecting focus priority for AF-S and AF-C reduces the number of out-of-focus pictures on your memory card.

By default, the camera is set to release priority, following the motto, "better a misfocused shot than no image at all." Since I am no friend of misfocused shots, my X-T10 is set to focus priority for both AF-S and AF-C.

Please note that when AF+MF is active in AF-S mode, the camera will always use AF-S Release Priority.

## 2.5 WHITE BALANCE AND JPEG PARAMETERS

A great feature of all X-series cameras is their ability to set white balance and JPEG parameters not only before you take a shot, but also after the fact using the built-in RAW converter. This gives you full control over the JPEGs that are generated in the camera.

- It's not necessary to anticipate and set the perfect settings for each shot in advance.

- You can generate different JPEG versions of a shot with the internal RAW converter. For example, you could create a version with bold Velvia colors, or a black-and-white version with strong contrast and minimal noise reduction.

It doesn't matter whether white balance and JPEG parameters are set before or after you take an image. As long as you have access to the RAW file, you can change all JPEG parameters after the fact and generate as many different-looking JPEGs as you want.

Using the built-in RAW converter in the playback menu is quite easy because it offers the same functions that are available in shooting mode (in the shooting menu and in the set-up menu).

| Shooting menu / Set-up menu | RAW Conversion menu |
| --- | --- |
| (Exposure Comp. Dial) | PUSH/PULL PROCESSING |
| DYNAMIC RANGE | DYNAMIC RANGE |
| FILM SIMULATION | FILM SIMULATION |
| WHITE BALANCE | WHITE BALANCE |
| (incl. WB SHIFT) | WB SHIFT |
| COLOR | COLOR |
| SHARPNESS | SHARPNESS |
| HIGHLIGHT TONE | HIGHLIGHT TONE |
| SHADOW TONE | SHADOW TONE |
| NOISE REDUCTION | NOISE REDUCTION |
| LENS MOD. OPTIMIZER | LENS MOD. OPTIMIZER |
| COLOR SPACE | COLOR SPACE |

The only relevant differences affect the first two items in this list:

- **Exposure corrections** made *before* you take a picture can affect aperture, shutter speed, and ISO. **Push/pull processing** *after* you have taken a picture only affects the ISO amplification. Changing the ISO via push/pull processing also doesn't change the ISO value in the EXIF data of the JPEGs. Push/pull processing in the internal RAW converter is the same as moving the exposure slider in external RAW conversion software such as Lightroom, Silkypix, or Capture One.

- *Before* you take an image, you can select four different **dynamic range** options: AUTO, DR100%, DR200%, or DR400%. DR200% exposes the RAW file one stop lower than normal; DR400% exposes it two stops lower. DR-Auto automatically selects either DR100% or DR200%. *After* you have taken an image, you can still select different DR settings in the internal RAW converter. However, you can only *reduce* the DR, not increase it. If you are working on a RAW file that was recorded with DR400%, you can reprocess it to create JPEGs with DR400%, DR200%, or DR100%. A DR200% RAW file can be reprocessed with DR200% or DR100%, but not DR400%. A DR100% RAW file can only be reprocessed with DR100%.

The correct **white balance** ensures that white or gray areas of an image appear white or gray (without color tints) regardless of the current light conditions. At the same time, the results are usually not supposed to look clinically neutral. The X-T10 masters this task quite well, so you can rely on the Auto white balance setting to get it right most of the time.

However, "most of the time" is not "all the time." There are instances when the white balance is off, or when you *want* it to be off. For example, you may want to emphasize a sunset with a warmer white balance, or maybe you want to take a whole series of shots at a certain location with the very same white balance for each shot. In such cases, it makes perfect sense to manually set the white balance in advance.

The X-T10 offers a variety of options to manually set the white balance:

- Seven white balance presets for typical situations, such as sunny weather (Fine), cloudy skies (Shade), or tungsten light (Incandescent)

- A Kelvin option to manually set the color temperature

- Custom white balance that actually meters a white or neutral surface (like a white wall) under the current light conditions. This way, the camera can adjust the white balance to make the surface appear neutral. The X-T10 offers three different slots to store custom white balance settings.

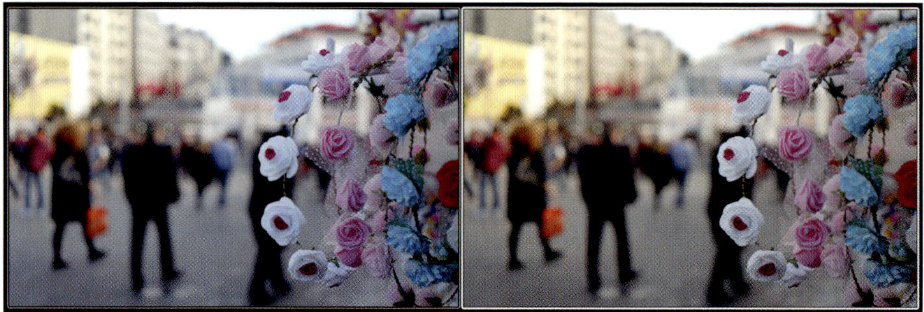

Fig. 50: Different **white balance settings** of the same shot: left: the (sometimes a little bit cool) Auto setting; right: the warmer Shade preset

| TIP 82 | **Custom white balance:** a little effort can go a long way |

This useful function is only available *before* you take a shot, because you are metering the white balance of the actual scene. Custom white balance allows you to calibrate the camera's white balance toward a specific object that you want to appear neutral in the final image.

Here we go:

- Select SHOOTING MENU > WHITE BALANCE > CUSTOM and press the RIGHT SELECTOR KEY (right arrow).

- Point the camera toward a surface that you want to use as a neutral reference, for example, a white wall or a gray card. Make sure that the surface is large enough to be fully covered by the white balance metering frame in the viewfinder. If that is not the case, come closer to your subject or zoom in.

- Fully press the shutter button to meter and set the new custom white balance. The live view will change accordingly and simulate the adjusted color temperature. If you are happy with the result, confirm it by pressing the OK button.

You can use the same procedure with a firing flash unit. In this case, the custom white balance will meter the mix of flash light and surrounding light that hits your neutral reference surface.

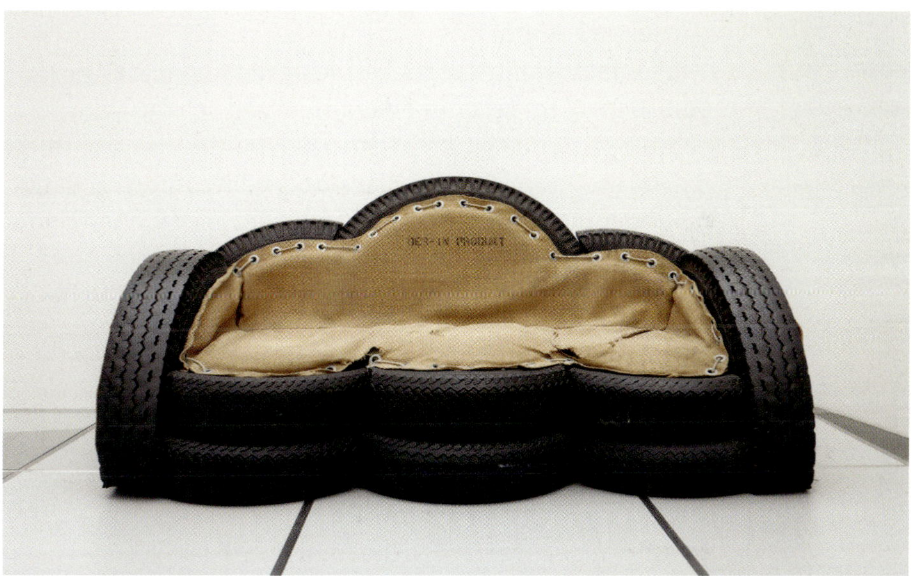

Fig. 51: A **custom white balance** setting was used to take this shot. The wall behind the sofa served as a neutral reference.

Don't worry! You are under no obligation to use the custom white balance later during RAW conversion. It's simply one of many options, and you can always adjust it later as you please. For example, you can use the built-in RAW converter with a manual KELVIN setting or one of seven white balance presets (FINE, SHADE, FLUORESCENT LIGHT 1–3, INCANDESCENT, and UNDERWATER). You can even use AUTO white balance anytime later because the camera will always save its automatic white balance metering for later use in the internal RAW converter.

| TIP 83 | Infrared photography |
|---|---|

Since the X-T10 features a rather weak IR-blocking filter in front of its sensor, it's quite suitable for infrared photography. You'll need an infrared filter in front of your lens, typically of the R72 kind, which is available from Hoya and other filter vendors. This filter blocks all light wavelengths except for infrared, making sure that only infrared light reaches the sensor.

In order to minimize the resulting red tint in the live view (and JPEGs), it's recommended that you set the color temperature to a minimum of 2500 Kelvin. You can also select one of the four different black-and-white film simulation modes to completely eliminate colors in the viewfinder (and JPEGs).

Since the R72 filter blocks a large amount of light, it's useful to shoot with a tripod.

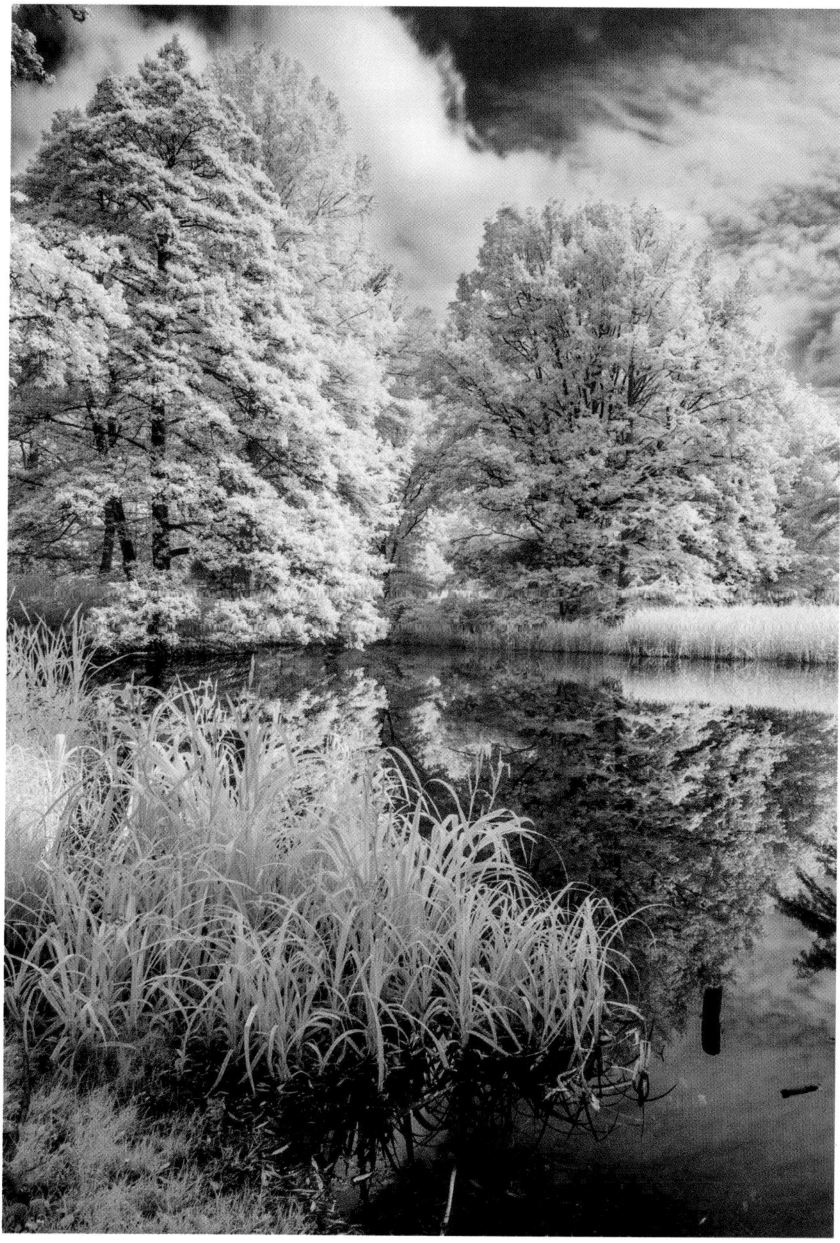

Fig. 52: This **infrared image** by X-Photographer Mehrdad Abedi was processed in Adobe Lightroom and shot with a Hoya R72 filter (Credit: www.qimago.de)

---

**TIP 84**  Changing color tints with **WB SHIFT**

---

WB SHIFT offers the opportunity to correct (or introduce) color tint to any shot. You can adjust the color tint as an add-on to every white balance setting—either before you take a shot, or in the built-in RAW converter.

You can set a *different* white balance shift for each of the X-T10's white balance options (Auto, Kelvin, the seven presets, and the Custom white balance). You can do this by changing the tint between green and red on the X-axis and between yellow and blue on the Y-axis of the display that automatically appears after you select one of the 12 white balance options.

I recommend a neutral setting here, especially since things can easily become confusing. As mentioned before, there's a different white balance shift setting for each of the 12 white balance options, meaning the camera can store 12 different white balance shift settings at once. This makes it easy to forget a previously set correction, which is why I recommend introducing white balance shift only after the fact during RAW conversion. Here's where you can actually see, for example, that the skin tones in a portrait may look too reddish and require an adjustment.

---

**TIP 85**  **Film simulations:** it's all about the look

---

The importance of film simulations for the overall look of a JPEG is often underestimated. Film simulations influence not just color grading but also color saturation, dynamic range, and contrast of the resulting JPEGs.

For this reason, picking a film simulation is always my first step when I'm adjusting JPEG parameters. As with all JPEG parameters, film simulations have no effect on the actual RAW file: the digital negative. Instead, they only affect the JPEGs that are generated in the camera: the digital prints. The X-T10 offers six different color film simulations, four black-and-white modes, and one sepia option:

- PROVIA is the standard, all-purpose setting of your X-T10. The name reminds us of Fuji's popular Provia slide film.

- ASTIA is another color slide film derivate with softer highlights and pleasing skin tones. It's often used for portraits, but can also work with landscape shots that feature a lot of vegetation. A special treat of this film simulation is its bluish shadows.

- VELVIA is a very contrast-heavy, color-saturated derivate of the legendary Fuji Velvia slide film. It's mostly used for landscape and nature shots and is definitely not the best choice for portrait work.

- CLASSIC CHROME is Fuji's latest film simulation. It has already become quite popular. That's understandable, since it reminds us of the golden era of *LIFE* magazine color photography. The distinctive look of Classic Chrome is equally suitable for landscapes and portraits.

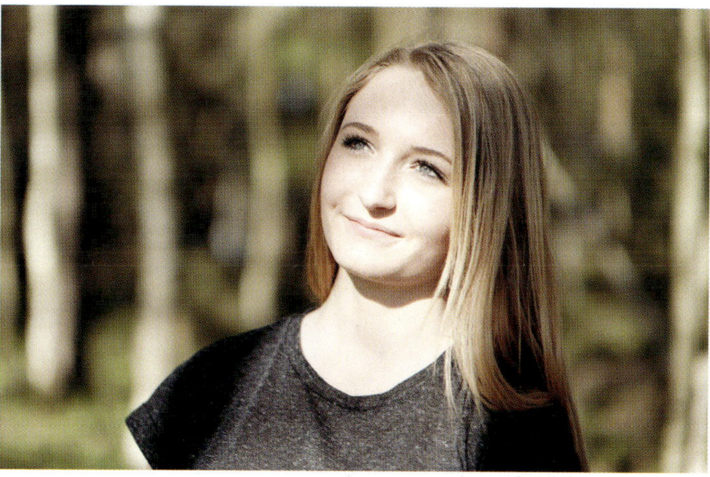

Fig. 53: The distinctive look of **CLASSIC CHROME** has earned it many fans in a very short time

- PRO NEG. HI is derived from a negative film that was specifically made for portraits. It delivers accurate and pleasing skin tones with nice contrast, adding some punch to the image.

- PRO NEG. STD is the most neutral film simulation of the X-T10. Featuring flat contrast, subdued colors, and high dynamic range, it can look dull at first, but the JPEGs are usable for further post-processing. Fuji recommends this film simulation for studio portraits in a flash setup.

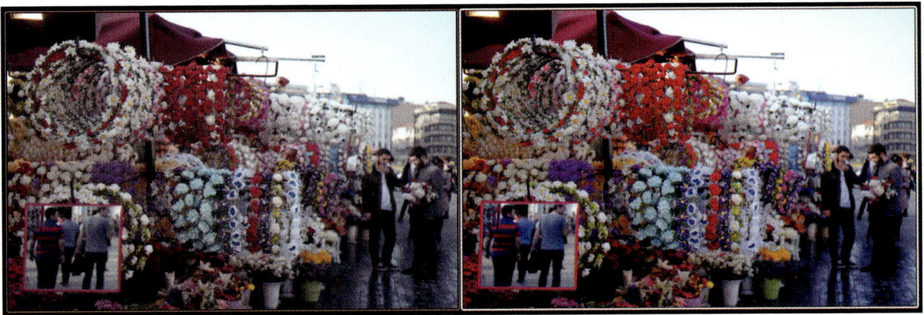

Fig. 54: **Antagonists:** PRO NEG. STD and VELVIA illustrate the bandwidth of Fuji's different film simulation modes. On the left you can see the PRO NEG. STD version of a shot, and on the right its VELVIA cousin.

- B&W is Fuji's standard black-and-white conversion. Black-and-white photography depends on different gray levels being assigned to different colors. In order to increase the contrast, many photographers combine B&W with increased SHADOW TONE and HIGHLIGHT TONE settings. Additionally, noise reduction is decreased to reveal more detail and display more noise that gives the appearance of film grain.

- MONOCHROME+Ye FILTER adds a digital yellow filter to the black-and-white conversion. This typically results in a slight increase of contrast because yellow parts of the color images will be represented by brighter gray tones.

- MONOCHROME+R FILTER adds a red filter to the black-and-white conversion. This means that skin tones will become brighter, which will camouflage reddish skin impurities. Conversely, blue skies will be darkened, adding contrast between clouds and the sky.

- MONOCHROME+G FILTER adds a green filter to the black-and-white conversion. This filter will add texture to skin tones and can potentially emphasize impurities.

- SEPIA results in a sepia-toned monochrome JPEG with an antique touch.

The best way to learn about film simulations is to use and compare the different options. The easiest way to do so is with the camera's internal RAW converter. Take the RAW file of a shot and process it with all available film simulations, then import the JPEGs into your computer and compare them on your monitor.

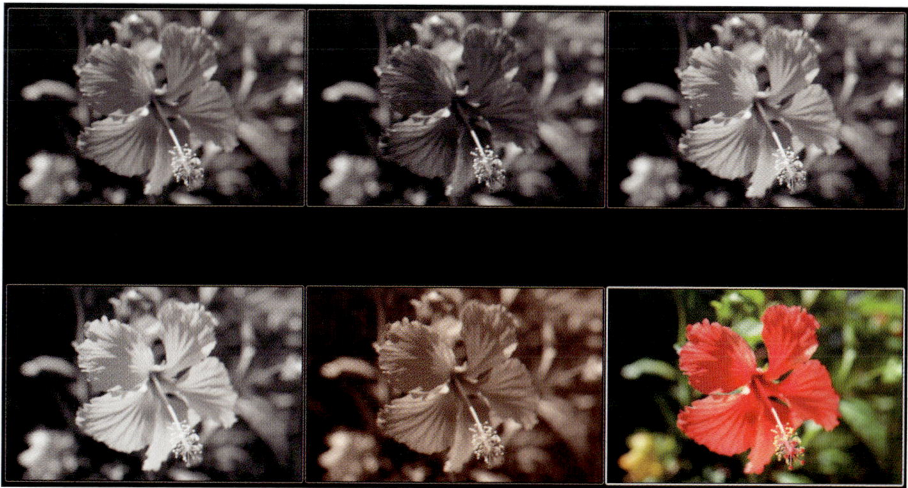

Fig. 55: **Comparing B&W options:** From left to right, first row: unfiltered B&W, green filter, and yellow filter. Second row: red filter, sepia, and the original shot in color.

| TIP 86 | **Contrast settings:** working with highlights and shadows |

A useful feature of the X-series is its ability to independently set the contrast for dark and bright parts of a JPEG image using the HIGHLIGHT TONE and SHADOW TONE settings. These settings can also be used to extend or reduce a JPEG's dynamic range by lifting dark shadows or darkening bright highlights.

To increase the overall contrast of a shot, you can increase both parameters at once by choosing a MEDIUM HARD or HARD setting. To reduce the overall contrast, pick a MEDIUM SOFT or SOFT setting for both parameters.

It's worth mentioning that increased contrast also enhances the impression of image sharpness and color saturation. This is important because it shows you that JPEG parameters can't be viewed isolated. They always work in concert with each other.

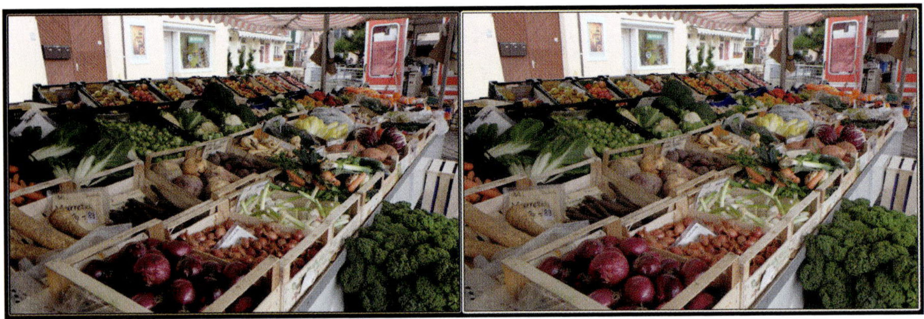

Fig. 56: Comparing **Shadow Tone** settings: The image on the left shows a SHADOW TONE 0 (standard) version; the image on the right shows the same RAW file processed with SHADOW TONE –2 (soft). As you can see, shadows and midtones are lifted up by the reduction of the JPEG's shadow contrast, while the highlights remain untouched.

---

**Skin tones:** smooth or with texture?                    TIP 87

---

The smoothness of surfaces (such as skin tones) at high ISO settings is best controlled by combining the SHARPNESS and NOISE REDUCTION parameters. To reveal more detail and achieve less skin smoothening, you can increase the sharpness to +1 (MEDIUM HARD) and decrease the noise reduction to −2 (LOW).

If this still doesn't meet your demands, you can switch to an external RAW converter to turn RAW files into JPEGs or TIFFs. Current versions of Adobe Lightroom/ACR and Iridient Developer offer good copies of the camera's internal film simulation modes. This means that you can replicate the famous Fuji Colors and enjoy more control over many processing parameters.

Please note that RAW files recorded with extended DR settings (DR200%, DR400%) may require additional processing when you use external RAW converters because you have to manually recover blown highlights using suitable exposure slider settings. The tone mapping is on you, because *you* are in control. In Lightroom and Adobe Camera Raw, you can combine the sliders for exposure, highlights, shadows, whites, and blacks to get the job done. In Iridient Developer, things are much simpler because this RAW converter offers a single Highlight Recovery slider with results that very much resemble the JPEGs from Fujifilm's internal DR function.

---

Color saturation                    TIP 88

---

After picking a suitable film simulation mode, you still might want to change the color saturation of an image. You can do so with the COLOR setting.

Too much color saturation can obscure texture and details, because at least one of the RGB color channels may be oversaturated. For example, VELVIA is a very saturated film mode that may sometimes require a reduction in color saturation.

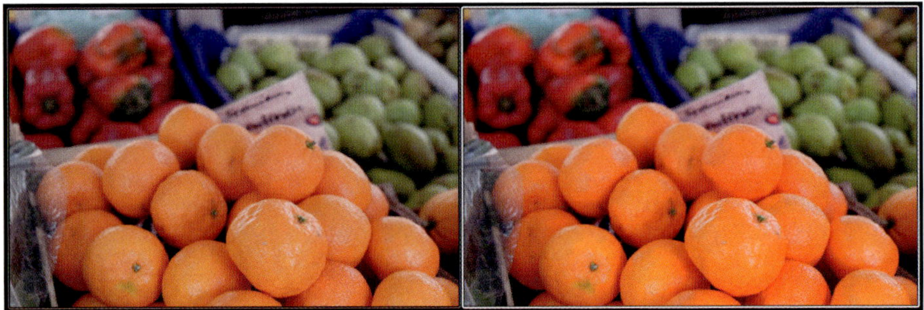

Fig. 57: **Color saturation:** The left image shows a version with COLOR –2; the right image show the same RAW file processed with COLOR +2

| TIP 89 | Choosing a **color space: sRGB or Adobe RGB?** |
| --- | --- |

A color space is a way of organizing available colors. Your X-T1o offers two options: sRGB and Adobe RGB. Both of these color spaces contain the same *number* of colors, but not the *same* colors—their gamuts are different.

Adobe RGB covers a larger gamut than sRGB because its colors are optimized for CMYK printing. On the other hand, sRGB is optimized for computer monitors and all kinds of high-resolution displays, such as HDTVs, smartphones, and tablets. Since Adobe RGB encompasses a wider gamut than sRGB, the gaps between neighboring colors and tones are wider because both color spaces contain the same number of colors. Adobe RGB has to spread this number over its larger gamut. This larger gamut (compared to standard sRGB) is why Adobe RGB is also known as an extended color space.

Users often misunderstand and assume that "extended" means "better." It does not. The additional colors in Adobe RGB are only useful if you intend to print images with a commercial CMYK printer. This requires a calibrated workflow and a wide-gamut monitor that is capable of displaying the Adobe RGB gamut. However, the vast majority of computer monitors are only capable of displaying the sRGB gamut. Using Adobe RGB on such a monitor would be like working with closed eyes because you wouldn't be able to see many of the colors you are dealing with.

For most users (including me), sRGB is the best choice of color space. Images rendered in this color space can be viewed, processed, and printed on a wide variety of devices without unpleasant surprises. In any case, you should calibrate your computer monitor with hardware like Spyder. Uncalibrated screens will not give you an accurate representation of the colors in your images.

| Using **custom settings** (usage profiles) | TIP 90 |
| --- | --- |

As you know, the X-T10 offers seven custom settings (or usage profiles) that can hold full sets of camera settings for quick access. The available settings are:

- ISO (incl. Auto-ISO 1–3)

- Dynamic range

- Film simulation

- White balance

- Color

- Sharpness

- Highlight tone

- Shadow tone

- Noise reduction

I'm sure you have noticed that these are the usual JPEG parameters with the addition of dynamic range.

The seven available custom settings (C1 to C7) or usage profiles aren't camera modes. They are just storage spaces for seven sets of settings than can be quickly retrieved (usually via the Quick menu) to replace the currently active camera settings. Custom settings are mere shortcuts, a simple time-saver that allows you to quickly change your camera's currently active settings as a whole instead of changing parameters one by one.

The best way of using custom settings is via the Quick menu:

- Pull up the Quick menu by pressing the Q button and select one of the seven available custom settings (C1 to C7).

- At this point, you can make changes to individual items of the retrieved parameter set using the Quick menu. Once you change a parameter, it is marked with a red dot.

- When you are happy with your settings and changes, you can make them your new current settings by pressing the OK button or by half-pressing the shutter button. In the upper-left section of the Quick menu, the currently active settings are always marked with the word BASE.

What kind of custom settings may be useful? Here are a few suggestions:

- Make sure to save your favorite all-purpose default settings in one of the seven user profiles (such as C1). This enables you to quickly revert to your default settings.

- Diehard RAW shooters can use a RAW shooter profile with dynamic range set to DR100%, HIGHLIGHT TONE −2, SHADOW TONE −2, and PRO NEG. STD film simulation.

- You could create profiles for black-and-white or infrared shooting. For example, a black-and-white profile could contain one of the four B&W film simulations, less noise reduction, additional sharpness, and additional highlight and shadow contrast.

To quickly edit custom settings, pull up the Quick menu, then press and hold the Q button again until the editing menu appears.

| Working with the built-in RAW converter | TIP 91 |
| --- | --- |

The RAW converter in your X-T10 serves two main purposes:

■ You can create different versions of a shot; for example, a colorful Velvia version and a gritty black-and-white version of the same image. Not sure what's best or what you want? Quickly create multiple versions with different film simulations and varying JPEG parameters, then sort them out later at home on your calibrated computer screen.

■ You can improve your JPEGs after the fact. Since it's hard (if not impossible) to set the perfect JPEG settings for each shot in advance, it's more convenient to adjust these parameters after the fact when you have time to look at your results. There's a good chance that you may be happy with many of your images, but if not, you can easily make adjustments to things like white balance, color saturation, contrast settings, sharpness, or noise reduction. You can also adjust the exposure and try different film simulations.

Here are a few things you can accomplish with the built-in RAW converter:

■ Use PUSH/PULL processing to brighten (push) underexposed shots or darken (pull) overexposed shots.

■ Use the contrast settings (SHADOW TONE and HIGH-LIGHT TONE) to selectively adjust the contrast of dark or bright parts of your image. It's perfectly adequate to combine these functions with PUSH/PULL processing. To generate JPEGs with maximum dynamic range for further post-processing on your computer, it may be useful to set both contrast parameters (shadows and highlights) to −2 (SOFT) and use a neutral film simulation like PRO NEG. STD.

- Adjust the color saturation of your JPEGs with the COLOR parameter. Reducing the color saturation can recover texture when one or more of the color channels appear oversaturated.

- Use SHARPNESS and NOISE REDUCTION in opposition with each other: increase sharpness while diminishing noise reduction to obtain more texture in high-ISO shots.

- Adjust the white balance using one of the presets or a Kelvin value to make your shot look warmer or cooler. Use WB SHIFT to correct or introduce a color tint.

- Want to know what the Lens Modulation Optimizer (LMO) is actually doing? Take a RAW sample and process JPEGs with and without LMO in the internal RAW converter. Then, compare the results on a computer screen. Happy pixel peeping!

- Picked the wrong color space? No problem! Just reprocess the shot with the right color space.

To process RAW files in your X-T10 that aren't stored on an SD card, you have to copy them back to a card and place them in the appropriate directory. If you are using a freshly formatted card, make sure to take at least one shot in order to create the X-T10's directory structure.

The directory where you must place your RAW files is located in a folder named DCIM. It's named "xxx_FUJI," with "xxx" being a 3-digit number that depends on the overall number of shots you have already taken. An example would be 104_FUJI.

Please remember that file transfers to the camera aren't available via USB, so make sure to insert the SD card directly into your computer or use a card reader.

By the way, your X-T10 cannot process RAW files from other camera models, including other X-series models. However, you can process RAW files from other X-T10 cameras. In this case, your camera will display a parcel symbol indicating that the RAW file was created with another X-T10.

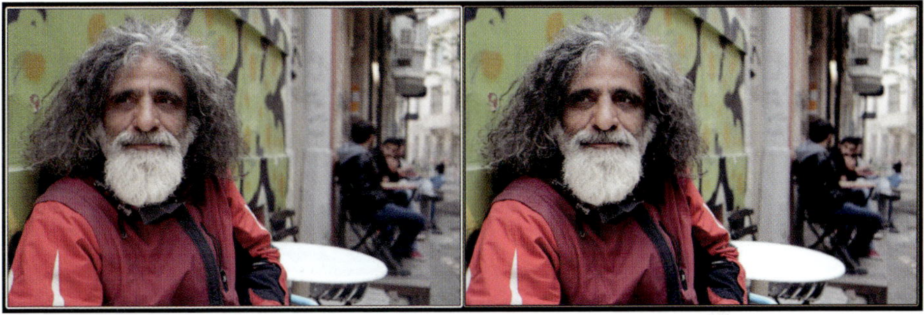

Fig. 58: The **built-in RAW converter** in action: The left image shows a sample shot that was processed with the camera's default settings and PRO NEG, STD. On the right, you can see the same shot processed with a PUSH of 1/3 EV, increased shadow contrast (SHADOW TONE +1), and decreased highlight contrast (HIGH-LIGHT TONE –1).

| Comparing RAW converters | TIP 92 |
| --- | --- |

So far, we have talked a lot about the built-in RAW converter of the X-T10. The internal RAW converter is the perfect tool to create JPEGs. It's a JPEG shooter's paradise! It's also super easy, because the built-in RAW converter utilizes the same functions and parameters that are available in the shooting menu. That's no surprise, because the built-in RAW converter *is* the JPEG engine of the camera! If you are a JPEG shooter, ignoring the internal converter that turns RAW files to in-camera JPEGs means overlooking the aspects of the camera that make the X-T10 so special. That's why even diehard JPEG fans are supposed to shoot with FINE+RAW. You need the RAW files to feed the engine that generates JPEGs with the colors, tonality, and overall look that you like from your Fuji camera.

Okay, enough already! What about the other half—diehard RAW shooters who don't care much about JPEGs, Fuji colors, or in-camera conversion? Those guys (and I tend to be one of them from time to time) require an external RAW converter to process the RAW files on a computer. The results are often saved as uncompressed 16-bit TIFF files of almost 100 MB each. Such files can be further processed in Photoshop and similar applications.

In this tip, I am going to compare popular external RAW processors with respect to how they handle specific features of the X-T10:

- **RAW File Converter EX** came free with your camera (have a look at the CD). This software is based on an older version of the Japanese **Silkypix** RAW processor that is currently available in version 6. If you want to use all the features of this software, you should definitely upgrade to the latest version of Silkypix. As a Fujifilm camera user, you are eligible for an upgrade discount in many places. Please note that the new RAW File Converter EX version 2 also supports Fujifilm's film simulation modes. This software is available as a free download from Fujifilm: www.fujifilm.com/support/digital_cameras/software/myfinepix_studio/rfc/.

- The most popular RAW converter is **Adobe Lightroom.** Its processing module is also available in Photoshop as **Adobe Camera Raw.** This website will provide more information and a free trial version: www.adobe.com/products/photoshop-lightroom.html.

- **Capture One Pro** is similar to Lightroom and deeply rooted in the professional community. It's made by PhaseOne, the same folks who are building medium format cameras and digital camera backs.

- A great RAW processor for Mac OS users is **Iridient Developer** from Iridient Digital. Like Lightroom/ACR, this converter features profiles that match Fuji's built-in film simulation modes.

- **Photo Ninja** from PictureCode is another fine option. Like Iridient Developer, it is able to extract a great amount of sharpness and detail from Fuji's X-Trans RAWs. It also contains a module for adaptive tone mapping and features a special algorithm to restore blown highlights.

Which RAW converter is right for you? I don't know! But I do know that you can download free trial versions of all mentioned programs to find out for yourself. That said, it can be helpful to make a quick comparison that tells you how well specific Fuji features are supported by each software.

Those features are:

- Original Fujifilm film simulations

- Exposures taken with extended DR settings (DR200%, DR400%)

- Digital lens corrections (distortion, vignetting, etc.)

Let's have a look...

FUJIFILM FILM SIMULATIONS

Provia, Astia, Velvia, Classic Chrome, Pro Neg. Hi, and Pro Neg. Std make up the color backbone of the X-T10. Together, they constitute the Fuji Colors. However, the makers of external third-party RAW converters often have their own ideas about the look of Fuji RAWs. Your mileage may vary, as they say.

- The **built-in RAW converter** is the benchmark reference for external RAW converters when it comes to emulating Fuji Colors.

- **RAW File Converter EX** and **Silkypix** feature a healthy amount of film emulations, but they all look different from Fuji's film modes. However, the new version 2 of the free RAW File Converter EX software *does* support Fuji's own film simulation modes for the X-T10. As of late October, 2015, these film simulations are also available in Silkypix 6.

■ **Adobe Lightroom** (version 5.4 and higher) and **Adobe Camera Raw** (version 8.4 and higher) feature camera profiles that closely emulate Fuji's film simulation modes—as long as you are shooting in DR100% mode.

■ **Capture One Pro** doesn't officially support Fuji's film modes, but it offers users the opportunity to create their own profiles. A few users have taken up the challenge, so you may find free film mode profiles in Fuji-related camera forums and blogs.

■ **Iridient Developer** now offers full support for Fuji's film simulation modes. Great stuff!

■ **Photo Ninja** doesn't support Fuji's film modes, yet. Boo!

EXTENDED DYNAMIC RANGE (DR200%, DR400%)
Using the DR function results in RAW files that are initially exposed 1 EV (DR200%) or 2 EV (DR400%) lower than normal in order to protect critical highlights. The darker exposure is compensated during RAW conversion by a partial ISO push of the same amount that only affects shadows and midtones.

■ The **built-in RAW converter** is the benchmark here, since it fully automates the tone-mapping process of partially pushing the shadows and midtones back where they belong.

■ **Silkypix** and **RAW File Converter EX** are smart citizens, too: they recognize RAW files with DR200% and DR400%, and they push them up by 1 or 2 EVs, then automatically recover the blown highlights by adjusting the highlight recovery slider accordingly. That said, the results don't necessarily look exactly like the JPEGs from the camera.

- **Lightroom** and **Adobe Camera Raw** are also smart enough to recognize RAWs with extended DR settings, and they automatically push the RAWs up 1 or 2 EVs when the images are opened with the software. However, recovering the highlights isn't an automated process; it's the user's job. Sadly, this can become pretty tedious because Lightroom's five exposure-related sliders work in a different way than Fuji's simple but effective tone mapping.

- **Capture One Pro** works just like Lightroom and applies a push of 1 or 2 EVs to RAWs that were recorded with a DR200% or DR400% setting. There's also a slider to recover highlights that may have disappeared during this push, but the results look different from Fuji's own DR tone mapping.

- **Iridient Developer** operates like Capture One, automatically pushing RAW files that were recorded with a DR200% or DR400% setting. There's also a Highlight Recovery slider to restore highlights that may have vanished, and here's the good news: the results very much resemble the look from the camera's internal RAW converter. Well done!

- **Photo Ninja** uses its own powerful adaptive tone-mapping module, and hence doesn't really bother emulating Fuji's simple tone mapping. There are several sliders to adjust a RAW file's exposure during processing.

## DIGITAL LENS CORRECTIONS

Digital lens corrections affect four areas: devignetting, distortion correction, removal of chromatic aberrations (CAs), and the Lens Modulation Optimizer (LMO). The information to perform such corrections is stored in the metadata of each RAW file. Every RAW converter can potentially read and use this metadata to apply appropriate image corrections. However, not all programs are able to do so.

- The **built-in RAW converter** supports all four types of lens correction. Note that some of Fuji's high-end prime lenses (like the XF14mmF2.8, XF23mmF1.4, XF35mmF1.4, and XF56mmF1.2) don't require digital distortion correction because they are already fully optically corrected. The LMO is only available in concert with XF lenses. XC lenses and Zeiss Touit lenses don't support the LMO.

- **Silkypix** and **RAW File Converter EX** can read and process the RAW metadata for distortion correction, devignetting, and CAs. All corrections are automatically applied and can't be controlled by the user. There is no LMO support.

- **Lightroom** and **Adobe Camera Raw** can also process lens-correction metadata and automatically apply the respective corrections in the background. It's currently not possible to control or stop the application of these lens corrections. However, it is possible to employ user-defined correction profiles that can be applied *in addition* to the automatic metadata application. It is not possible to *replace* metadata with user-defined corrections. There is no LMO support.

- **Capture One Pro** can also process lens-correction metadata. Unlike Lightroom and Silkypix, it allows the user to control the intensity of the corrections or switch them off altogether. There is no LMO support.

- **Iridient Developer** can use lens-correction metadata, too. Like Capture One, it also provides full control over the extent of the corrections. There is no LMO support.

- **Photo Ninja** ignores all lens-correction metadata. Instead, the software asks the user to provide suitable profiles or to manually correct distortion, vignetting, and CAs.

Automatic lens metadata corrections can look a bit different depending on the RAW converter because each converter tends to interpret the data differently.

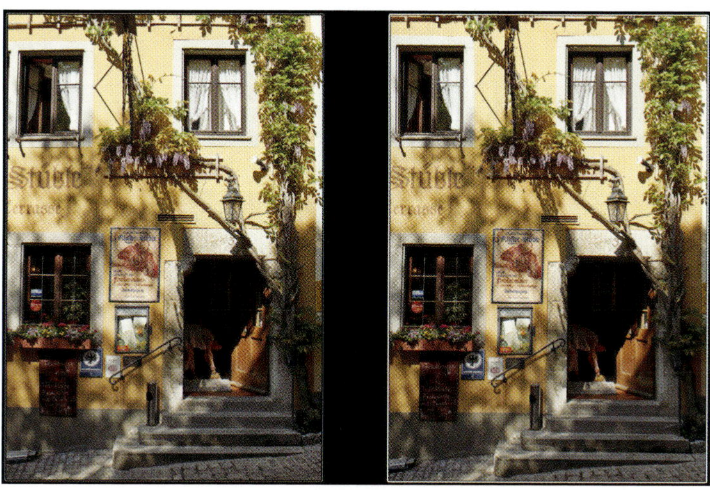

Fig. 59: **Digital lens correction:** This shot was taken with a Zeiss Touit 1.8/32 lens. The left image shows the shot in Capture One Pro without digital distortion correction. On the right, you can see how Capture One Pro applied the digital distortion correction to straighten the lines.

| Displaying EXIF metadata | TIP 93 |
| --- | --- |

Digital cameras save information about every recorded image in the EXIF data of each RAW or JPEG file. This data can be useful to RAW converters and cataloging software, but it can also be useful to you to help you understand how an image was exposed.

EXIF data consists of information about exposure parameters, camera settings, date and time, focal length, AF settings, white balance, JPEG parameters, DR mode, digital lens correction data, serial numbers of cameras and lenses, etc. Many of these data points are saved in an area called "maker notes," which contains information on camera features that are specific to a certain brand (like Fujifilm). Exif-Tool can read the EXIF data and is also able to make sense of maker notes. ExifTool is rarely standalone. Instead, you can get it as part of other image utilities, such as ExifTool GUI for Windows or GraphicConverter for Mac OS users.

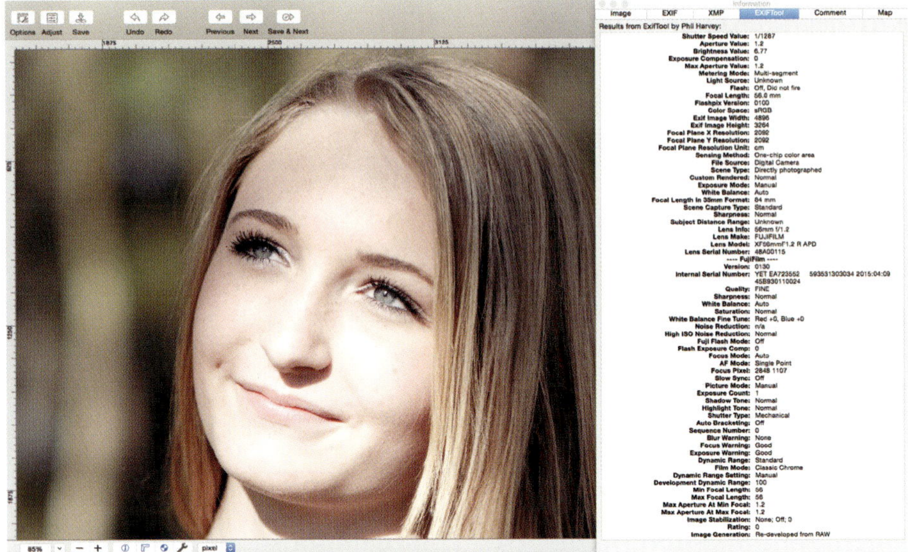

Fig. 60: **EXIF** data of an X-T10 shot in GraphicConverter: There's a vast amount of information about every image, including brand-specific Fujifilm maker notes

## 2.6 BURST MODE, MOTION PANORAMA, MOVIES, AND THE SELF-TIMER

The DRIVE dial of your X-T10 gives access to several modes and functions that control bracketing options, burst shooting, panorama mode, etc.

Some of the bracketing options (set DRIVE dial to BKT1 or BKT2) are only available in JPEG mode, so those of us who shoot FINE+RAW will never use them:

- Film simulation bracketing

- ISO bracketing

- DR bracketing

Due to technical reasons, advanced Filters, Multiple Exposure, and Motion Panorama don't save RAW files, either:

■ ADVANCED FILTER (set DRIVE dial to ADV.1 or ADV.2) offers a variety of special effects. Most of them are gimmicks, but give them a try and see what they can do for you!

■ MULTIPLE EXPOSURE is actually just a double exposure and a rather simple feature that merges two consecutively taken JPEGs. Usually, it's better to perform this in software like Photoshop.

■ MOTION PANORAMA is a nice feature that automatically takes and stitches panorama shots.

<table>
<tr><td>Using burst mode</td><td>TIP 94</td></tr>
</table>

In burst mode, the camera takes a quick sequence of shots while you press and hold the shutter button. The X-T10 offers two speed settings: CL (3 fps) and CH (8 fps). In principle, both speeds work in the same way:

■ White balance, autofocus, DR settings, and exposure (aperture, shutter speed, ISO) are determined for the first frame of the series and then carried over to all consecutive shots. This means that all shots of the series have the same white balance, autofocus, DR settings, and exposure.

■ As usual, there's one exception: using AF-C in concert with burst shooting, the camera will refocus (track) before each frame and also adjust the exposure of each shot. However, white balance and DR settings are still carried over from the first frame of the series.

<table>
<tr><td>TIP 95</td><td>Shooting **motion panoramas**</td></tr>
</table>

MOTION PANORAMA is a derivate of burst mode: while you pan the camera in a horizontal or vertical motion, the X-T10 takes a series of images and stitches them together into a panoramic JPEG file. You can choose between two sizes (M and L), and you can specify the direction of your panning motion (left, right, up, and down).

The maximum size of a motion panorama is 7680×2160 pixels. It's available when you choose size L and a vertical motion. Of course, you can use a vertical motion horizontally by holding the camera upright.

Here are a few tips for getting the best results with motion panoramas:

- Since MOTION PANORAMA results in only a JPEG file (no RAW), JPEG parameters such as white balance and film simulation have to be set *before* taking the shots.

- White balance and focusing remain constant during the recording of a motion panorama. This applies to all focus modes (AF-S, AF-C, and MF). That's why it's important to set a focus distance and depth of field that work for the entire panoramic scene.

- Panoramas tend to extend over a wide area with varying light conditions and strong changes in contrast. In such cases, it's smart to shoot with an extended DR setting, such as DR200% or DR400%. In addition to that, the exposure should be set in a way that suits the entire panoramic image, not just a small part of it. The edges of a panorama are rarely representative; it's usually better to base your exposure on the main part of the image in the middle. Motion panorama works with all four exposure modes, so shooting it in manual mode **M** may be the smartest option. Please note that motion panorama only works with multi metering.

- If you decide to *not* manually set exposure, white balance, and focus, point the camera toward a representative part of the panoramic scene, then lock focus, exposure, white balance, and DR by half-pressing the shutter button. Then pan to the point where you'd like to start the panning action (while holding the shutter button half-depressed), press the shutter button fully, and start panning.

- Avoid scenes that contain a lot of motion. Moving objects (people, vehicles, etc.) can lead to ghosting artifacts, which is when moving objects (partially) appear in more than one spot of the final panorama.

- Keep a healthy distance from the panoramic scene. Don't shoot panoramas in close quarters. Also make sure that you have sufficient depth of field. Wide-angle lenses are better suited for this job than normal or telephoto lenses.

- Always pan with the EVF (camera held to your eye), not with the LCD display (arms stretched in front of you).

- While panning, stand parallel to the panoramic scene and always stand on level ground.

- Try to ignore the time delay that may occur between the currently recorded image and what's displayed in the EVF. Keep panning the camera in a smooth motion until the camera stops taking frames.

- Vertical banding in the final JPEG can indicate that the shutter speed was too fast. In this case, try again with a slower shutter speed.

- Use a tripod and make sure the camera is leveled to the horizon.

- Immediately check your finished panorama in the camera's viewfinder after you have captured it. Look out for stitching errors and ghosting artifacts. Do this while you are still on location, not at home when it's too late to reshoot a panorama that went wrong.

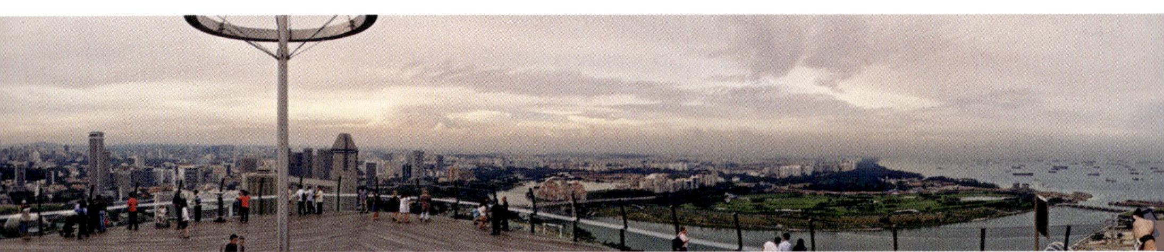

Fig. 61:  A standard **motion panorama:** The camera automatically takes as many frames as it needs to stitch the panoramic JPEG image. Watch out for ghosting artifacts! They are present in this sample image and hard to avoid when the scene contains objects that move around during the panning action.

| TIP 96 | **Shooting video** with the X-T10 |
| --- | --- |

Pressing the video recording button for about a second makes the X-T10 record videos in HD quality. You can choose between Full HD (1920×1080 pixels) and a lesser HD resolution (1280×720 pixels). Both resolutions are available with 24, 25, 30, 50, or 60 frames per second.

- MOVIE mode is available in concert with all four **exposure modes** (**P**, **A**, **S**, **M**), so you can change both aperture and shutter speed *before* and *during* recording. However, you can't change the exposure mode during a recording. There's also full manual ISO control between ISO 400 and ISO 6400 *before* you start recording. Auto-ISO is supported, too. In this case, the camera will automatically select ISO settings between 400 and 3200. Your current Auto-ISO configuration for still photography (default sensitivity, max. sensitivity, min. shutter speed) is ignored in video mode. Strangely, ISO 200 is not available in the X-T10's video mode, and ISO for video recording can only be set with SHOOTING MENU > MOVIE SET-UP > MOVIE ISO, not in the normal ISO menu. Please note that the shutter speed can never be slower than the selected frame rate. For example, at 60fps, the shutter speed has to be 1/60s or faster.

- The only **exposure metering** mode available in video mode is multi metering. In modes P, A, and S, the camera automatically adjusts the exposure during video recording. However, you can bias the exposure with the camera's exposure compensation dial before and during recording within a range of ±2 EV.

- **Focusing** is possible with all three modes: AF-S, AF-C, and MF. You can also switch modes during filming. AF-S sets the focus before recording starts, so there's no AF tracking during video recording. AF-C continuously adjusts the focus during video recording, always targeting the center of the screen. In MF mode, you can adjust the focus with the focus ring before or during video recording. One-Touch-AF (Instant AF) is available, but only before you start recording.

- **Face detection** is also available in movie mode, controlling the focus and exposure of the scene. Beyond that, face detection operates like AF-C, so it's continuously adjusting focus and exposure with respect to the detected face closest to the center of the scene.

- Sadly, there is no support for the **DR function** in video mode. There also are no "zebras" or "blinkies" to mark overexposed areas. You have to trust the live view (there is no live histogram during video recording) and adjust the exposure as necessary.

- With automatic **white balance** (AUTO), the X-T10 is continuously adjusting the white balance during video recording. You can also use one of the white balance presets or a Kelvin setting. Custom white balance is available, too.

- You can adjust the look of your videos by selecting one of the camera's 11 **film simulations**. That's it. Contrast or color settings don't have an effect.

- In movie mode, the X-T10 is also recording **audio**. You can either use the built-in stereo microphone or attach an external microphone. The latter is recommended if you don't want to record camera sounds like the AF motor or aperture changes. An external microphone is available from Fujifilm, but you can also use third-party offerings. The latter require a 3.5mm to 2.5mm adapter in order to fit into Fuji's microphone socket. Using an external microphone also requires you to set SHOOTING MENU > MOVIE SET-UP > MIC/REMOTE RELEASE > MIC. Otherwise, the camera will think that you are using a remote shutter release. You can adjust the sensitivity of the audio recording with the MIC LEVEL ADJUSTMENT menu option.

- Using a lens with **optical image stabilization** (OIS) reduces camera shake during video recording. Just make sure that the OIS is switched on.

<table><tr><td>TIP 97</td><td>Using the self-timer</td></tr></table>

The camera's built-in self-timer delays the shutter release (exposure) after you press the shutter button. This function isn't available on the DRIVE dial; you have to find it in the shooting menu (or the Quick menu). You can select one of two delay options:

- A 10-second delay is typically used when you want to make sure that you are also in the picture when the shot is taken. Press the shutter button and run.

- A 2-second delay replaces a remote shutter release when you are working on a tripod. The delay helps the camera to settle down, so there's no camera shake or vibration when the actual exposure begins.

## 2.7 FLASH PHOTOGRAPHY

Flash photography means taking a double exposure. A flash shot always consists of two components that are merged into one: **surrounding light** and **flash light**.

- The **surrounding-light** component is metered like a regular exposure. The camera is metering the scene with multi, average, or spot metering, while the exposure mode (**P**, **A**, or **S**) automatically selects suitable exposure parameters based on your adjustment of the exposure compensation dial. As usual, the live view and live histogram are your friends. Of course, you can also set the exposure of the surrounding-light component manually in mode **M**. Basically, exposing the surrounding-light component works exactly like exposing a scene without flash at all.

- The **flash-light** component is automatically metered and adjusted by the camera to match the overall exposure. To accomplish this, the X-T10 employs a so-called TTL metering system. TTL stands for Through The Lens. It means that the flash light is entering the camera through the lens before it's metered with the image sensor. This happens with the help of a weak preflash that is emitted solely for metering purposes. You can bias the strength of the automatic flash-light component either with FLASH COMPENSATION in the shooting menu, or directly on some external Fujifilm TTL flash units like the EF-20 or EF-X20. Please note that while the live view and live histogram provide a preview of the surrounding-light component, they completely ignore the flash-light component that will be added to the final image.

Besides the built-in TTL flash or external Fuji and Fuji-compatible TTL flash units, you can also use third-party flash units. Pretty much everything that fits onto the hot shoe works. Using generic third-party flash units means that TTL flash metering is no longer available, so you must manually set the flash energy output. You can also use automatic flash units that use their own built-in light sensor to automatically measure and adjust the flash output.

*Important: This chapter is based on X-T10 firmware version 1. Since Fuji has already promised to enhance the flash functionality of the X-T10 in 2016 (for instance, offering wireless TTL with support for different groups or flash photography in burst mode), it's possible that your camera already offers additional flash photography features at the time you read this book. If that's the case, please have a look at my* X-Pert Corner *blog (www.fujirumors.com/category/x-pert/), where I will be covering new firmware features.*

The TTL flash logic in your X-T10 supports several flash modes that can be selected in the Quick menu or in SHOOTING MENU > FLASH SET-UP > FLASH MODE:

- AUTO is only available in mode **P** and automatically fires an available flash unit if the camera decides it's necessary. It's a silly mode, since you probably know better than your camera whether or not you want to use a flash light.

- FORCED FLASH always fires an active flash unit. This setting is available in all of the four exposure modes (**P**, **A**, **S**, and **M**).

- SLOW SYNCHRO works like FORCED FLASH, but allows shutter speeds as long as 1/8s to better capture the surrounding-light component. This can be helpful when the light is poor and you still want to capture more of the background. This setting is only available in modes **P** and **A**.

- 2ND CURTAIN SYNC works like FORCED FLASH, but fires the flash when the shutter is closing. This is relevant for shooting moving subjects at slow shutter speeds. Since flash photography is a double exposure, it makes a difference whether the flash is fired at the beginning or at the end of a longer exposure. This setting is available in all four exposure modes (P, A, S, and M).

■ COMMANDER is a trigger flash that optically releases other external flash units (or slaves) that feature an optical sensor. This function is available in Fuji's EF-X20 and several third-party flash units. Please note that you have to manually adjust the power of the triggered slave flash. Don't forget that the commander flash is also emitting flash light that can affect the exposure of your scene, especially when you are shooting with high ISO settings. Personally, I prefer triggering remote flash units with a wireless radio transmitter or a Canon OC-E3-compatible flash extension cable. The latter even allows using the camera's TTL functions. Commander is available in all four exposure modes (P, A, S, and M).

■ SUPPRESSED FLASH makes sure that no flash is fired, even when the flash is switched on and connected to the camera.

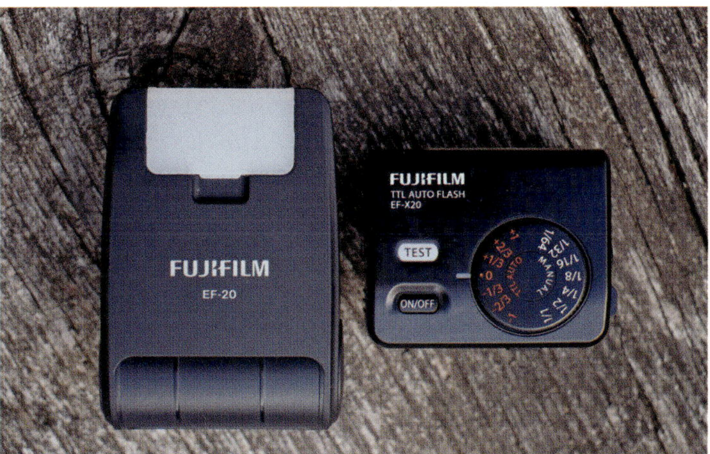


Fig. 62: A sizeable difference—comparing **TTL system flash units** EF-X20 and EF-20: Both options offer about the same flash power and are a reasonable fit on your X-T10 when the power of the camera's built-in flash isn't sufficient

> **TIP 98** | **Flash photography in modes P and A:** slow shutter speed limits

In modes **P** and **A**, the camera automatically selects suitable shutter speeds to capture the surrounding-light component of the scene.

- In flash modes FORCED FLASH, 2ND CURTAIN SYNC, and COMMANDER, the slowest available shutter speed is the reciprocal of the focal length divided by 2. For example, shooting with a 55mm focal length, the slowest available shutter speed will be 1/55s / 2 = 1/110s. This is a hard limit. Another hard limit in these modes is 1/30s. No matter what focal length is in use, the camera will never use a slower shutter speed than that. These hard limits mean that the surrounding-light component (basically the background) of the shot can end up underexposed. There are exceptions, though. *Exception number 1:* Lenses with built-in and active OIS ignore the reciprocal rule and only follow the hard minimal shutter speed limit of 1/30s (or 1/15s when OIS + motion detection is active). *Exception number 2:* Auto-ISO can overrule both shutter speed limits for flash photography (the reciprocal limit and the 1/30s or 1/15s minimum) if you set a slower minimum shutter speed in Auto-ISO, such as 1/15, 1/8, or 1/4s. To achieve even slower shutter speeds in concert with flash photography, you should use mode **S** or **M**.

- SLOW SYNCHRO allows the camera to use slower minimum shutter speeds with flash photography. There's only one hard limit of 1/8s, which is independent from the focal length or an active OIS. To achieve even slower shutter speeds, you should use mode **S** or **M**.

<table>
<tr><td>Controlling the surrounding-light component of flash photography</td><td>TIP 99</td></tr>
</table>

When you are metering a scene with your X-T10, you will quickly realize that it doesn't make any difference whether the flash is turned on or off while doing so. The metering result will always be the same. In other words, the X-T10 is always metering the surrounding-light component in the same way, with or without flash. In case you choose to use a flash, the flash-light component will simply be *added* to the surrounding-light component.

This is important because it tells us that we don't have to fear some camera voodoo that may or may not influence the metering of the surrounding light as soon as we switch on a flash. Instead, we can be sure that the camera's metering will always deliver consistent results. Shooting with flash won't change the metering. This also means that it's our job to balance both components, for example by reducing the surrounding-light components to make room for more flash light in the composite exposure.

Typically, if you want to use the flash as a fill-in light to brighten a dark foreground (such as a backlit person), you wouldn't have to change much, since the flash-light component would brighten the dark foreground simply by filling in the light that's missing. However, if you use the flash on a scene that's already correctly exposed by natural light, the camera's TTL flash metering would come to the conclusion that no additional light is needed. The forced flash would still fire, of course, but with minimal output; it will probably be almost invisible in the resulting shot. In order to emphasize the flash-light component, reduce the exposure of the surrounding-light component.

Here's how it works:

- You can control the exposure of the surrounding-light component either with the exposure compensation dial or by setting an appropriate manual exposure (ISO, aperture, shutter speed). Less surrounding light will prompt the TTL flash metering to add a stronger flash-light component, since the TTL flash system will always try to deliver balanced results. Changing the exposure compensation dial has no effect on the flash component of the shot; it only affects the exposure of the surrounding-light components.

- To control the surrounding-light components in manual mode **M** using the live view and the live histogram, make sure to set SET-UP > SCREEN SET-UP > PREVIEW EXP. IN MANUAL MODE > ON.

- In a studio, you often want to minimize the surrounding-light component and illuminate your subject entirely with flash light. In such cases, I recommend small aperture settings (large aperture numbers), base ISO 200, and a fast shutter speed. The fastest official flash synchronization speed of the X-T10 is 1/180s, but some flash units allow you to go faster, up to 1/250s. In order to view such a scene with little surrounding light in mode **M**, set SET-UP > SCREEN SET-UP > PREVIEW EXP. IN MANUAL MODE > OFF. Otherwise, it will be hard to see anything in the viewfinder other than darkness.

- Sometime the fastest flash sync speed (1/180s) will still overexpose the surrounding-light component, even at base ISO 200. Sure, you could stop down the aperture, but this might negate the purpose of achieving a nice subject-to-background separation with little depth of field. In such a case, it's useful to attach a neutral density filter to the lens to reduce the amount of light that hits the sensor by 3 to 6 stops.

- Similar to the DR function, flash light is often used to reduce contrast between a dark subject and a bright background. You can combine both features, which may be useful if the background—when viewed isolated from the foreground—still contains so much contrast that DR expansion is required. Think of a night scene with city lights, streetlamps, billboards, etc. in the background. In such a scenario, a flash light could illuminate a person standing in the foreground, while the DR function (DR400%) would help capture the colors and textures of the city lights.

- The previously discussed, hard minimum shutter speed limits in modes P and A can lead to an underexposed surrounding-light component. However, these limits are quite useful because they prevent shaky or blurred backgrounds in handheld shots. This isn't an issue when using a tripod, so you could circumvent the limits by selecting SLOW SYNCHRO or by manually setting a slow shutter speed in S or M mode.

- Surrounding light and flash light frequently exhibit different color temperatures, which makes it difficult to find a white balance setting that suits all parts of the image. Luckily, some RAW converters (like Lightroom) allow selective white balance editing in an image. Another method is to use a gel filter in front of the flash unit to warm or cool the flash light to better match the surrounding light.

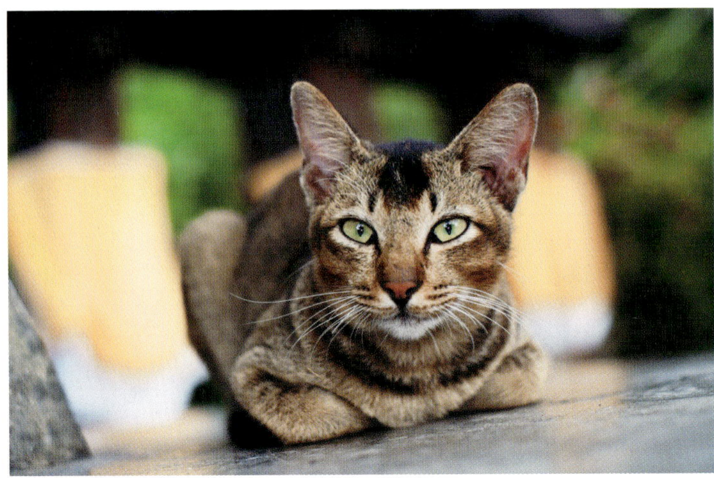

Fig. 63: With plenty of surrounding light, the flash-light component takes a backseat. In this example it simply added a spark to the cat's eyes. The best flash-light shots are often those that aren't easy to identify as flash photography.

| TIP 100 | Controlling the flash-light component |
| --- | --- |

If the flash-light component of your image turns out too bright or dark, you can bias the camera's TTL flash system:

- To bias the flash-light component of your shot, you can adjust the flash exposure compensation in the camera (SHOOTING MENU > FLASH SET-UP > FLASH COMPENSATION) or on your external TTL flash unit (EF-20, EF-X20, or EF-42). Combining the in-camera flash compensation with an additional compensation setting on the flash unit itself will simply add up both corrections.

- You will often get nicer-looking results by bouncing the flash off the ceiling, which makes the flash light look softer and more natural. Of course, bouncing the flash light requires much more power, so you may need a stronger flash. It's also worth noting that bouncing the flash from a colored surface will tint the light accordingly.

- To add a tint or change the color temperature of your flash light, you can attach colored gel filters in front of your reflector. The color temperature of unfiltered flash light usually corresponds to regular daylight.

- The range of your flash unit depends on the set aperture, the ISO setting, and (of course) the power setting. In TTL mode, the camera is automatically adjusting the light output of your flash, but many flash units can also be set to manual so you are the one setting the power output of the flash. In manual mode **M**, changing the shutter speed doesn't affect the brightness of the flash-light component of your shot. Hence, changing the shutter speed is a quick way to adjust the exposure of the sur-rounding-light component without messing with your carefully balanced manual flash-light setup.

- Don't forget that large lenses and lens hoods can block parts of the flash, resulting in unpleasant shadows. It's better to remove the lens hood or to use off-camera flash.

- Some wide-angle lenses cover a larger angle of view than the reflector of your flash. This results in unpleasant vignetting. In such cases, bouncing the flash light off the ceiling can be helpful. Alternatively, you can attach a diffusor to the flash reflector. Many flash units feature built-in diffusors—just don't forget to flip it on.

| | |
|---|---|
| **2nd curtain flash synchronization:** what's the deal? | TIP 101 |

Flash photographs are double exposures consisting of surrounding light and flash light. When you shoot the surrounding light with a slow shutter speed, there is the question of when the flash (with its much faster shutter speed) should fire. Normally, the flash is fired at the *beginning* of an exposure when the shutter curtain opens. However, se-lecting 2ND CURTAIN SYNC. makes the flash fire at the *end* of the exposure when the shutter curtain closes.

Naturally, moving objects change their position during the exposure of a shot. Synchronizing the flash with the second curtain ensures that it's "freezing" moving objects where they are at the end of the exposure as opposed to the beginning. This often results in the moving object appearing more natural in the image.

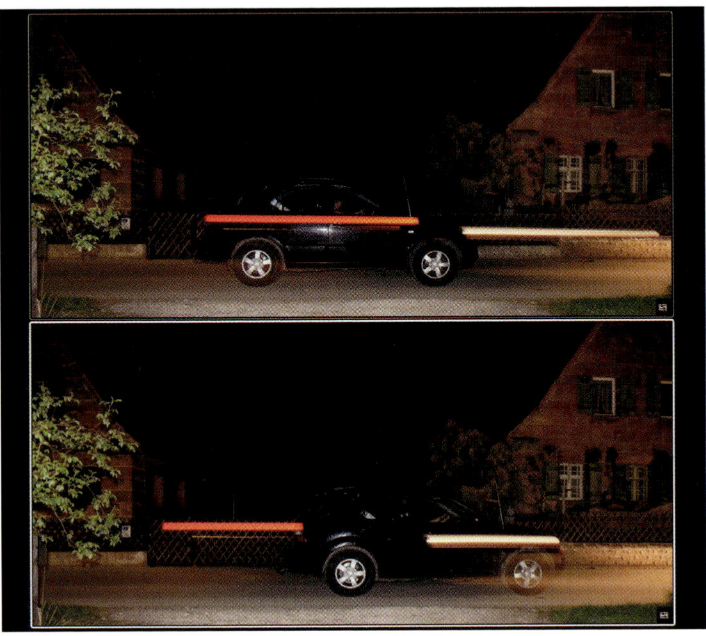

Fig. 64: **First vs. second curtain sync:** This examples shows the same scene photographed with first curtain sync (above) and second curtain sync (below). The shot above shows how the flash freezes the moving vehicle at the beginning of the exposure while the shot below shows it being frozen at the end of the exposure. The second-curtain version looks more natural and avoids the false impression of the car moving backward. This is also a good example to examine in terms of the nature of flash photographs as double exposures. You can see how the slow shutter speed captures the moving vehicle as a blurry trail of light, while the fast flash instantly freezes parts of it.

<table><tr><td>Flash synchronization: where's the limit?</td><td>TIP 102</td></tr></table>

Officially, the fastest flash sync speed of the X-T10 is 1/180s.

- In exposure modes **P** and **A**, the camera will never offer a shutter speed faster than 1/180s. If this is too slow for the current light conditions, the surrounding-light component will be overexposed. In this case, the shutter speed of 1/180s will be displayed in red. To avoid overexposure, stop down the lens, reduce ISO (but never below 200), or use a neutral density (ND) filter in front of the lens.

- In exposure modes **S** and **M**, you are able to select shutter speeds faster than 1/180s. The X-T10 will honor these settings in flash mode, but there will be a price to pay: the resulting images will display some partial shadowing of the flash. It's often possible to use shutter speeds as fast as 1/200s or 1/250s without visible negative effects. It very much depends on the type of flash you are using. Its power setting plays a role, as well. Proceed at your own risk!

- High-speed synchronization (HSS) is currently not supported by the X-T10.

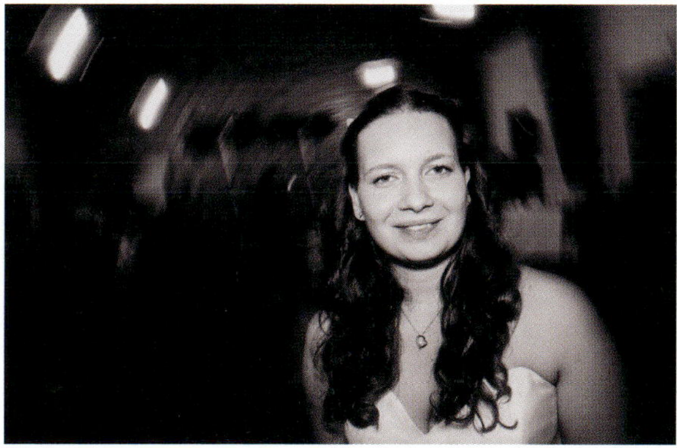

Fig. 65: Many photographers wish to use a flash sync speed faster than 1/180s with their X-T10. That said, it's possible to deliberately use very slow sync speeds to create a blurry background behind a more contoured flash-lit foreground.

<table><tr><td>TIP 103</td><td>**Red-eye removal:** a two-step affair</td></tr></table>

If the flash and your subject share (almost) the same optical axis, this can lead to the red-eye effect: an unpleasant red reflection in the eyes of humans or animals.

- If you activate SHOOTING MENU > FLASH SET-UP > RED EYE REMOVAL in concert with FACE DETECTION in the shooting menu, the camera will emit a preflash prior to each shot that forces your subject's pupils to contract, thus reducing or eliminating the red-eye effect. There will be no preflash if face detection is turned off.

- Independently, there's *another* red-eye removal tool available in the camera's playback menu. PLAYBACK MENU > RED EYE REMOVAL performs face detection in the captured JPEG file and automatically retouches red eyes via image processing. If you want to keep a copy of the unretouched JPEG, set SET-UP > SAVE DATA SET-UP > SAVE ORG IMAGE > ON. The RAW file isn't affected by this variant of red-eye removal.

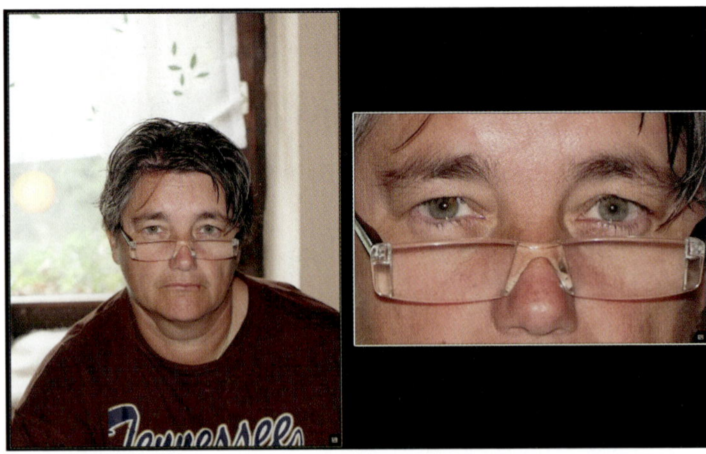

Fig. 66:  The **red-eye removal** function in the X-T10 emits a preflash that is bright enough to prompt your subject's pupils to contract. This example shows a crop of the actual image.

<table><tr><td>Little slave: the EF-X20</td><td>TIP 104</td></tr></table>

Fuji's TTL system flash EF-X20 was specifically made for retro-style cameras like the X-T10. Besides using it as a TTL flash, you can also set its output power manually. You can even trigger it wirelessly with another flash, such as the camera's Commander flash.

- Set the flash mode in your X-T10 to COMMANDER.

- Move the mode switch on your EF-X20 to the N position.

- Manually set the desired flash output on your EF-X20. There are seven levels, from 1/1 (full power) to 1/64.

When you take an image with your X-T10, the flash on your camera will now wirelessly trigger the EF-X20. Please take into account that the light emitted by the commander flash can still affect your image.

Fig. 67: An optically triggered **EF-X20** slave flash

<table><tr><td>TIP 105</td><td>Silent Mode, a.k.a. SOUND & FLASH OFF</td></tr></table>

The camera's so-called Silent Mode has been renamed SOUND & FLASH OFF in the X-T10 (SET-UP > SOUND & FLASH OFF). This mode not only mutes all the artificial sounds (beeps, clicks, etc.) of your X-T10, it also suppresses light emissions such as flash light, the AF illuminator, or the self-timer indicator.

Sound & Flash Off is basically a stealth mode for situations that temporarily require you to shoot very discreetly. To get rid of all sounds for good, select SET-UP > SOUND SET-UP > OPERATION VOL. > OFF.

Please note that the sound of the mechanical shutter is real. You can't get rid of it. However, the sound of the electronic shutter is artificial and can be controlled and muted in the SOUND SET-UP menu.

<table><tr><td>TIP 106</td><td>Using third-party flash units</td></tr></table>

Basically, you can use any modern flash unit from any vendor with your X-T10, as long as you are prepared to manually set its power. You can connect third-party flash units directly to the camera's hot shoe, or use a cable or a wireless (radio) triggering device.

The camera's TTL modes aren't available when you are using third-party flashes because the camera isn't *metering* the flash light, it's only *triggering* the flash. Again, the maximum sync shutter speed is 1/180s. Unofficially, faster sync speeds up to 1/250s may sometimes be possible.

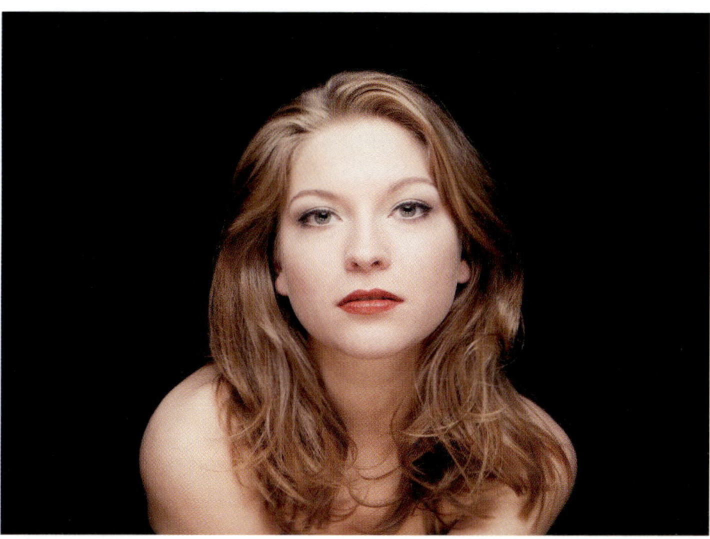

**Fig. 68:** Manually controlled **studio flash shot** using an Elinchrom Ranger Quadra

## 2.8 USING ADAPTED LENSES

Thanks to its short flange-back distance, the X-mount system is able to host almost every existing full-frame, medium format, or APS-C lens. All you need is an appropriate adapter ring. This means that in addition to more than a dozen native lenses, you have access to hundreds of additional modern and legacy lenses.

| Finding the right **lens adapter** | TIP 107 |
| --- | --- |

X-mount lens adapters are available for many old and current mounts. Here are a few tips to help you find the right adapter for your third-party lens:

- Adapters are available at many price and quality levels, and the "you get what you pay for" rule does apply. Don't buy too cheap or you may end up buying twice. The German manufacturer Novoflex is setting the benchmark here, but their adapters can be more expensive than the lens you are adapting. Asian manufacturers like Kipon or Metabones enjoy a good reputation, and they all offer adapters for a wide variety of lens mounts.

- Adapted lenses can only be used as manual focus lenses. There is currently no electronic adapter that can translate between Fuji's AF protocol and the AF protocols of popular brands like Canon or Nikon.

- All adapted lenses use manual aperture settings and always operate with a manually set working aperture. This means that when you are stopping down the lens, the live view and live histogram of your X-T10 have to contend with the set aperture's reduced amount of light. It also means that adapted lenses can only be used in exposure modes **A** or **M**.

- Many modern third-party lenses that don't feature a manual aperture ring can still be mechanically adapted to your X-T10, but you can't change their aperture while they are connected to your camera via an adapter. That's why some adapters feature a mechanical replacement aperture, but the results produced by these devices will differ from the results created by the original lens.

- Modern electronic features like optical image stabilization (OIS) aren't supported since there is no communication between the X-T10 and the adapted lens. In fact, the camera believes that there's no lens attached at all.

- *Speed Booster Ultra* from Metabones offers an amazing possibility to attach full-frame lenses from Contax/Zeiss, Canon FD, Nikon G, Minolta MD, and Leica R to the X-T10 without changing their angle of view or cropping the image on your camera's APS-C sensor. Basically, your APS-C camera sees what a full-frame camera would see. Speed Booster is a reduction adapter—basically the opposite of a teleconverter. It reduces the focal length of the adapted lens by a factor of 0.71. At the same time, the brightness (speed) of the lens is increased by about one stop. At 400–600 dollars apiece, Speed Booster adapters aren't cheap. However, they offer much better quality than knock-off products like the Lens Turbo by Zhongyi Mitakon.

■ Fujifilm offers its own adapter for Leica M-type full-frame lenses. This is a regular adapter (no Speed Booster), but it features electronic contacts so the camera will recognize it. It also features an Fn button that provides direct access to the camera's MOUNT ADAPTOR SETTING menu. With all other adapters, you have to set SHOOTING MENU > SHOOT WITHOUT LENS > ON in order to take a picture.

■ Caution: don't use cheap macro lens adapters with electronic contacts. These cheap adapters are designed to serve as macro spacer rings for native X-mount lenses. They promise full AF functionality thanks to their electronic X-mount contacts. In reality, these adapter rings can be a very bad fit and can damage your camera and lenses. Instead, I recommend using Fuji's own electronic macro extension tubes MCEX-11 and MCEX-16.

■ Never try to combine more than one adapter. Stacking adapters leads to a measurable and visible loss in quality. Instead, get the right adapter for your lens.

| Adapting third-party lenses: here's how... | TIP 108 |
| --- | --- |

When you connect third-party lenses to your camera via an adapter, the camera won't notice it due to the lack of electronic contacts. The X-T10 will think there's no lens attached at all. The only exception is using Fuji's own Leica M-mount adapter.

- In order to make the camera work with adapted lenses, set SHOOTING MENU > SHOOT WITHOUT LENS > ON.

- Enter the focal length of your adapted lens in the SHOOT-ING MENU > MOUNT ADAPTOR SETTING menu. You can either select the focal length from one of four presets or enter it manually in LENS 5 or LENS 6. Always enter the actual focal length of a lens (as it is printed on the lens), not its full-frame equivalent for APS-C cameras. This ensures that the EXIF data will display the correct focal length.

| TIP 109 | Exposing with adapted lenses |
| --- | --- |

Adapted lenses can be used in exposure modes **A** (aperture priority) and **M** (manual mode). There are also a few notable differences between exposing with native lenses and adaptive lenses:

- Native lenses close to working aperture only when the shutter is half-pressed. Adapted lenses always operate with the aperture set by the user. As soon as you stop down an adapted lens, less light reaches the sensor and the camera's exposure metering.

- Stopping down also increases the depth of field in the viewfinder. Since less light reaches the sensor, the camera has to more strongly amplify the live view image in order to display an accurate WYSIWYG simulation of the scene. This decreases the quality of the live view image and can also negatively affect the live view's frame rate.

- Since the camera thinks there's no lens attached at all, the aperture is always displayed as F0 in the viewfinder. There's no way for the camera to know which aperture has actually been set on an adapted lens.

■ Shooting in poor light with adapted lenses can become tricky when you stop down the aperture. It's easy to reach the live view's amplification limit. Once this limit is reached, the live view and live histogram cannot display the actual brightness of the scene, so it appears darker than the image that will be actually exposed. However, exposure metering will still work correctly and the camera will display the correct shutter speed. In mode **M**, the ±3 EV light scale in the display will also work correctly.

■ Since the electronic viewfinder cannot control the aperture of an adapted lens, it takes longer for the camera to adjust to abrupt brightness changes. You can test this yourself by quickly panning the camera from a bright scene to a dark scene and vice versa. With adapted lenses, the camera will need a few seconds for the live view to adapt to the changing brightness levels.

| Focusing with adapted lenses | TIP 110 |
|---|---|

Adapted lenses can only be focused manually. Here are a few tips to make things easier for you:

■ Set the focus selector of your X-T10 to manual focus. This makes sure that MF assistants such as focus check, focus peaking, and digital split image are available.

■ The electronic distance and depth-of-field (DOF) scale of your X-T10 is useless in concert with adapted lenses. Instead, you have to rely on analog scales and markers that may be engraved on the barrel of your adapted lens. Remember that the DOF scale on your lens is probably less conservative than what you are used to from the electronic scale in your X-T10 and will not guarantee pixel-sharp results at 100% magnification.

■ The most important tool for focusing with adapted lenses is the magnifier tool, also known as focus check.

You can activate it by pressing the rear command dial. Turn the rear command dial to cycle between two available magnifications. Don't forget: instead of focusing and recomposing, it's better to select a magnifier frame that covers the part of the image you want to be in focus. You can move the magnifier frame by pressing the AF button and then using the selector buttons (arrow keys) to move the frame around the 49 available positions.

- Use focus peaking or digital split image. You can cycle between these MF assistants and the standard view by pressing and holding the rear command dial. The magnifier tool can be combined with focus peaking and digital split image. However, in concert with digital split image, only one magnification level is available.

- The magnifier tool (focus check) and MF assistants work best at wide-open aperture, when the DOF is as small as possible. However, some lenses exhibit so-called focus shift, meaning that the focus plane shifts backward when the lens is stopped down. In such cases, the increased DOF from stopping down the lens may not be sufficient to compensate for the focus shift, so your carefully focused shot will end up out of focus when the aperture is closed. If you are using a lens with focus shift, it's better to focus with the actual working aperture instead of the wide-open aperture. Please note that focus shift isn't a matter of price—even a few high-end lenses from Leica and Zeiss suffer from it.

| TIP 111 | Using the **Fujifilm M-mount adapter** |

Fuji's own M-mount adapter is a little bit different from conventional adapters:

- The adapter features electronic XF lens contacts to identify itself to the camera. However, there's no transmission of any lens data since the adapter doesn't know which M-type lens has been attached or what distance and aperture has been set. Sadly, the electronic contacts also make the inner adapter tube thinner than normal, so not all M-type lenses are physically compatible with it. This website (www.fujifilm.com/products/digital_cameras/accessories/lens/mount/fujifilm_m_mount_adapter/compatibility_chart/index.html) has a list of compatible and incompatible lenses. Fuji is enclosing a template with its M adapter that you can use to find out if your M lens measures up with the adapter.

■ Pressing the function button on the adapter directly opens the camera's adapter menu.

■ The adapter menu offers a few additional functions when a Fuji M-mount adapter is attached. In addition to entering the focal length, you can also enter correction values for lens distortion, color shading, and vignetting. Those corrections only affect the JPEGs during RAW conversion with the built-in or external RAW converters. As usual, the corrections are burned into the RAW file metadata where they can be interpreted by RAW conversion software. However, color-shade data is currently only processed by the camera's built-in converter. For each adapted lens, you have to find out the right correction values for yourself before you can enter them. There aren't any reference lists you can use that I know of.

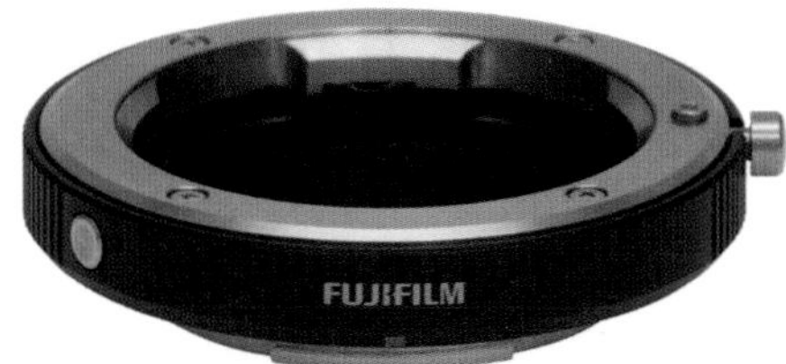

Fig. 69: Fujifilm's own **M-mount adapter** features electronic contacts and a function button that opens the camera's adapter menu

<table><tr><td>TIP 112</td><td>Quality considerations</td></tr></table>

Pixel peeping is en vogue, but many classic lenses rooted in the area of analog film weren't made for high-resolution digital sensors. While some very expensive Leica lenses may be outright disappointing when used on an X-T10, some really cheap old lenses can deliver excellent results.

How can we explain that?

The lens design plays a major role. Some compact lenses (typically for M-mount cameras) feature a symmetrical design that tends to be more problematic with digital sensors than telecentric SLR designs.

Also note that most adapted lenses are intended for full-frame cameras. Attached to an X-T10 with its smaller APS-C sensor (23, 7×15, 6mm), the format of the lens is cropped. If one would extend the size of Fuji's 16-MP sensor to full-frame (36×24mm), its resolution would be 36 megapixels, just like the Nikon D810 or Sony's A7r. Obviously, there aren't many older full-frame lenses that can actually use this kind of resolution. Instead, many older lenses offer something else: character. Because maximum sharpness and resolution weren't as important then as they are today, the designers of legacy lenses could put their priorities elsewhere, for example by designing lenses that provide outstanding bokeh.

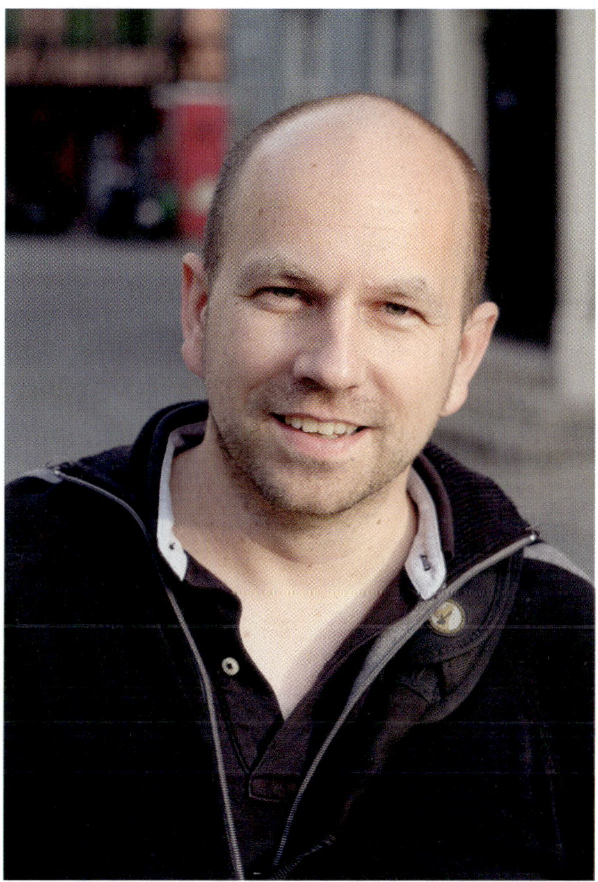

Fig. 70:  Good legacy lenses don't have to be expensive: this shot was taken with a Russian **Helios 44M-4,** a 58mmF2 lens with an M42 screw mount. You can often find this lens online for less than $25. In fact, the Novoflex adapter to attach the lens to the X-T10 cost me much more than that.

| **Speed Booster:** miracle or trick? | TIP 113 |
| --- | --- |

Speed Booster and Speed Booster Ultra from Metabones are very special adapters. They convert the focal lengths of full-frame lenses to their APS-C equivalents. This means that the adapted lens covers the same angle of view on your X-T10 as it would on a full-frame camera.

Take my *Carl Zeiss Sonnar T* 2.8/180 MM* as an example. It's a classic telephoto lens with a Contax/Yashica full-frame mount. Adapting this lens to my X-T10 *without* Speed Booster causes the results to look like images taken with a 270mmF4.2 lens on a full-frame camera. That's because there is a crop factor of 1.5 between full-frame and APS-C.

Of course, many users of full-frame lenses would like to use them on a smaller APS-C camera like the X-T10, yet keep the angle of view and depth of field constant. Speed Booster can do that for you because it reduces the focal length of the adapted lens by a factor of 0.71. With Speed Booster, my 2.8/180mm full-frame Sonnar turns into a 2/128mm APS-C lens.

Is there a price to pay? Well, yes, since Speed Booster isn't cheap. With regards to image quality, the MTF of the new lens is actually improved, but there's a chance of vignetting when Speed Booster is used to adapt fast lenses. That said, the new Speed Booster Ultra improves vignetting issues that were problematic with the original Speed Booster. In any case, Speed Booster is better than knock-off products such as Lens Turbo.

Speed Booster increases the speed (or maximum aperture) of a lens by about one stop, so you can use faster shutter speeds or lower ISO settings. For example, let's assume you need ISO 800 to shoot a scene with your full-frame DSLR at f/2.8 (wide open) with a 180mm lens and 1/1000s. On the X-T10, Speed Booster turns this lens into a 128mmF2 lens with the same angle of view. Shooting wide open (now f/2) at 1/1000s, you can drop the ISO to 400. Since full-frame sensors tend to offer an ISO advantage of about one stop over APS-C, the results from both cameras should be equivalent, because the X-T10 sensor can compensate its smaller size by applying 1 EV less ISO amplification.

Speed Booster is available for several classic mounts, such as Canon FD, Nikon G, Contax/Yashica (Zeiss), Minolta MD, Contarex, ALPA, and Leica R. Sadly, there is no Speed Booster for Leica M, because an M adapter would be too thin to house the necessary optics.

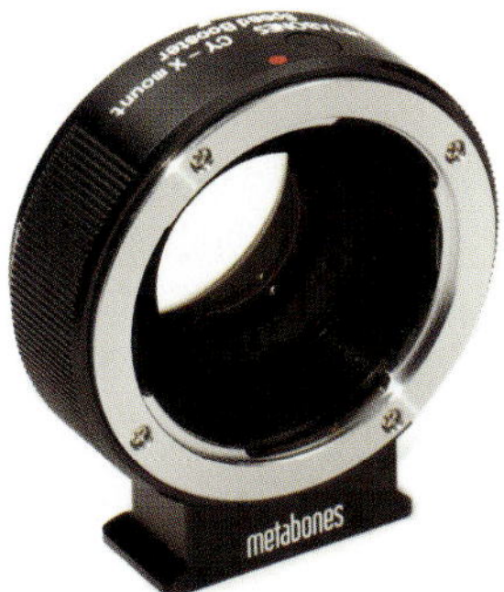

Fig. 71:  Metabones **Speed Booster** with Contax mount

## 2.9  WIRELESS REMOTE CONTROL

Fuji's own Camera Remote app works with wireless iOS and Android devices, and it allows you to remotely control your camera by providing a live view image and a touch-screen interface to set the focus point, change exposure parameters, and take a shot.

| Using the **Camera Remote App** | TIP 114 |
| --- | --- |

Camera Remote allows you to control the X-T10 from an Android or iOS device running Fuji's Cam Remote app. The wireless connection is based on the camera's or smartphone's Wi-fi capabilities.

In order to use Camera Remote, you have to download and install the free Cam Remote app on your smartphone or tablet. You can find download links, instructions, and additional information at the following website: app.fujifilm-dsc.com/en/camera_remote/index.html.

***Important:*** *Make sure that you use the **Cam Remote App** and not the older **Camera App**.*

Here's how Camera Remote works with iOS devices (and it shouldn't be much different for Android users):

- Select SHOOTING MENU > WIRELESS COMMUNICATION on your camera. The X-T10 now enters wireless mode and emits a Wi-fi signal.

- Hook up your smartphone's or tablet's Wi-fi with the camera's Wi-fi network. Each camera comes with a unique network name that you can customize in SET-UP > CONNECTION SETTING > WIRELESS SETTINGS > GENERAL SETTINGS > NAME.

- Open the Cam Remote app and select Remote Control. The mobile device will now assume control over the camera and display a live view image along with options to adjust shutter speed, aperture, or exposure compensation. There's also a virtual shutter button and a small shooting menu that allows you to adjust parameters like ISO, film simulation, white balance, macro, flash mode, or self-timer.

- In order to autofocus on a specific part of the live view image, double-tap with your finger on it. Focus will be confirmed with a green rectangle, and the camera will issue a confirmation beep. If no focus lock can be established, the rectangle will appear in red.

- Adjust your exposure parameters as required. The brightness of the live view will change accordingly. Please note that there's no live histogram.

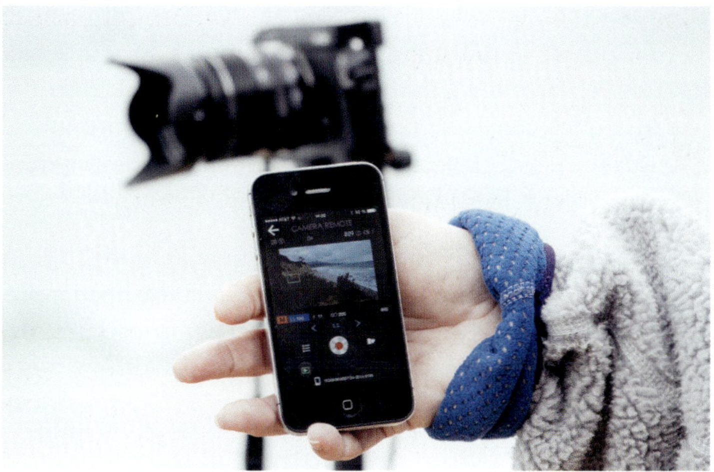

Fig. 72: Camera Remote offers a simple interface to control your camera with a smartphone or tablet. To autofocus, double-tap on a specific part of the WYSIWYG live view and wait for the green confirmation rectangle to appear. Sadly, there is no live histogram, and you can't magnify the live view. There is a rudimentary shooting menu, a virtual shutter button, and a playback button that allows you to review images and transfer JPEGs to your mobile device.

Here are a few things you might want to know about Camera Remote:

■ Fuji's Camera Remote app allows you to adjust exposure parameters (aperture, shutter speed, ISO, exposure compensation), but you can't remotely change the camera's exposure mode. This means that you have to manually set the camera to either **P**, **A**, **S**, or **M** mode *before* you select WIRELESS COMMUNICATION in the shooting menu. In order to change the exposure mode during remote shooting, you have to first disconnect Camera Remote, make the desired changes in the camera, and then start over with a new connection as directed above.

■ There's no electronic level indicator and no live histogram in the Camera Remote live view on your mobile device.

- You can change several shooting parameters from within the Camera Remote app (ISO, film simulation, white balance preset, macro, flash mode, self-timer), but other parameters (such as dynamic range or Auto-ISO minimum shutter speed) have to be preset in the camera before entering wireless communication mode.

- There is no bulb functionality in Camera Remote, so your maximum exposure time is 30 seconds. If you need more, it's better to use a conventional (tethered or wireless) remote shutter release.

- The X-T10 also allows you to shoot video with Camera Remote.

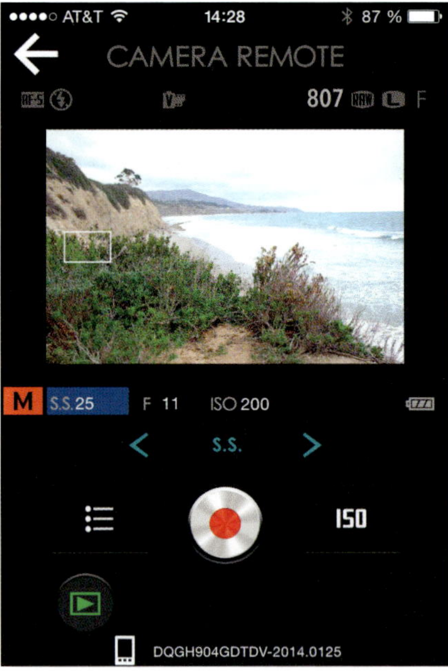


Fig. 73: Changing exposure parameters affects the WYSIWYG live view. In the above image, I changed the shutter speed to 1/25s, and the resulting overexposure is quite visible in the iPhone's display. The live view always reflects the currently selected film simulation and JPEG parameters. Like in the X-T10 itself, there is no preview of the DR function.

A few more tips and hints:

- I use Camera Remote mostly in manual exposure mode **M**; I feel that this is the most convenient and efficient way to adjust shooting parameters. Changing a parameter (shutter speed, aperture, ISO) immediately adjusts the live view brightness.

- iOS users may be annoyed by the need to frequently reconnect the smartphone to the camera's Wi-fi network, since the connection has to be dropped and reestablished for every mode or parameter change made in the camera. This can be particularly cumbersome at home, where the iOS device is automatically reconnecting with your home network as soon as the camera has been disconnected.

- Android users (particularly Sony users) may suffer from connection losses caused by interfering networks that are transmitting on the same Wi-fi channel as the camera. Sadly, there is currently no way to change the camera's transmission channel. As an iOS user, I haven't experienced any such difficulties yet.

- In order to transfer JPEGs from the camera to your mobile device with full 16-MP resolution, make sure to select SET-UP > CONNECTION SETTING > WIRELESS SETTINGS > RESIZE IMAGE FOR SMARTPHONE > OFF. Otherwise, the transferred images will be downsized to 3 megapixels.

- Manual DR extension settings (DR200%, DR400%) are not reflected in the Camera Remote live view of the X-T10. Setting the X-T10 to Natural Live View (PREVIEW PIC. EFFECT OFF) is also not reflected in the Camera Remote live view. JPEG parameters such as contrast (HIGHLIGHT TONE, SHADOW TONE) or white balance settings are fully reflected, though, and in manual mode **M**, the Camera Remote live view will also respect any settings made in SET-UP > SCREEN SET-UP > PREVIEW EXP. IN MANUAL MODE.

- Wi-fi drains the battery, so you better pack spare batteries or use Fuji's CP-W126 DC DC coupler and AC-9V power adapter to connect the X-T10 to an external power source.

Besides remote controlling the X-T10, the Camera Remote app offers additional functions that allow you to transfer JPEGs from the camera to your mobile device (one by one or in groups of up to 30 shots) and to copy GPS location data from your smartphone or tablet to the camera.

## 2.10  ANYTHING ELSE?

Hopefully, this book was able to answer many of your questions that went beyond the manual of your camera. However, this isn't the end: you can read my *X-Pert Corner* blog, participate in Fuji X forums, or join one of my Fuji X Secrets workshops.

| TIP 115 | **Forums, blogs, and workshops:** be a part of it! |

- High-resolution versions of selected images in this book are available in this Flickr album: https://www.flickr.com/gp/25805910@N05/20L4L8.

- My free *X-Pert Corner* blog covers a variety of topics about the Fujifilm X series. You will find everything from service articles that go beyond this book to First Look previews of new cameras and lenses. You can read *X-Pert Corner* here on Fujirumors: www.fujirumors.com/category/x-pert/.

- There are several online forums that focus on Fujifilm's X series: The Original Fuji X Forum (www.fujix-forum.com), The Ultimate Fuji X Forum (www.fuji-x-forum.com), the Fuji X-Series Forum (www.fujixseries.com), and FujiX-

Spot (www.fujixspot.com). The latter forum contains a special section where I'm personally available to answer questions or discuss Fuji X-related issues.

- For questions and comments that you don't want to post in public, you can contact me at rico@ricopress.de. Use this subject line: The Fujifilm X-T10: 115 X-Pert Tips.

- Books, blogs, and forums are great, but what about a more personal touch? Fuji X Secrets (www.fuji-x-secrets.com) is a series of advanced workshops for Fuji X-series users. My workshops cover topics that are similar to those in this book, but on a more in-depth level, including practical demonstrations and plenty of sample images. We work in small groups, and our delegates set the agenda. It's everything you always wanted to know about X, but were afraid to ask. We are also organizing travel workshops to great photo locations: In 2015, we went to Istanbul, and in November 2016, we will host an exclusive weeklong Fuji X Secrets workshop in Phuket, Thailand.

# INDEX

# Don't close the book on us yet!

Interested in learning more on the art and craft of photography? Looking for tips and tricks to share with friends? For updates on new titles, access to free downloads, blog posts, our eBook store, and so much more visit rockynook.com/information/newsletter

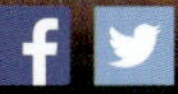


rockynook